TO:
DIVA TAFFY Fie...

Everyone should
Have A
TAFFY

LC's Take
~
Poetry
I

in
Their
Lives —

Cool Calm wise —
+ oh, WHAT A
wRiter!

LC

9/1998

LC's Take

~

Poetry
I

LC Van Savage

Custom Communications/Publisher
Saco, Maine

DEDICATION

I dedicate this book of poems to my two best friends,
husband Stephen and sister Betsy; two people who have
always said about everything I've ever wanted to do or
dreamed of doing to "Go for it!" I did!

Published by Custom Communications, 92 Franklin St., Saco, ME 04072
(207) 286–9295. E-mail: custom@desktoppub.com.
Web site:http://www.desktoppub.com

Library of Congress Cataloging-in-Publication Data
Van Savage, LC, 1938–
LC's take. Poetry I / LC Van Savage. —1st ed.
     p.   cm.
ISBN 1-892168-03-0
1. Humorous poetry, American. I. Title.
PS3572.A537L18   1998   98–36371
811'.54—dc21   CIP

Design, Typography, and Setup
Custom Communications
First Edition
Printed in the United States of America.
10 9 8 7 6 5 4 3 2 1

TABLE OF CONTENTS

252	9
Scared Or Afraid??	10
Clay	11
Circles Within Circles Within...	13
Clusters	15
Learning	15
Life Is—	16
Crickets	17
Brussels Sprouts Etc.	17
Me and My Cicadas	20
But Not in the Back Yard	21
'Bye Bill	22
Ibid Who?	23
Learning	23
The Burned House	24
White Dream	27
A to Z Color Me	28
Fire and What?	32
Be Great	33
Anymore	35
The Berry Boy	36
The Banana	37
The Story of Doc and Kay	38
Ann Was A Fool	40
Wyeth and Dot	41
Imbibing	44
Even Then Stuff Caught in Teeth Was Gross	45
Elephants	46
What's In a Name? What's Not?	49
Yum	51
Emma	52
Falling Stars, Dying Stars	53

Birthday Greetings to Fred Stewart 56
Squirrels 58
My Flower 58
Sorry 61
G Before L 61
Needles and Leaves 63
My Ghost 64
My Jungle 68
Oh No, YOU Tell Him 70
Final Wishes 70
Fireflies 71
Money 72
Soap Mysteries 73
The Horse on the Ribbon 74
Out, Damned Splinter 75
In A Word 76
O Way Down South in Loozyanna 77
If 78
Women in Pants, Men in Skirts 79
My Lake 81
My Way of Exercising 82
From Lebanon With Love 83
Lenora Lee 85
Those One Shoes 87
Nails 88
Little Girls 88
Men on Vacation 90
Sister Bernadette Gets Down! 91
Hats and Moi 94
My Prayer 95
Orange Oranges 96
The Sister and Her Rainbow 96
Bob and I and the Plaza 99
In Praise Of 103
The Lady's Clothes Man 104
Men and Plaids 104

The Peanutbutter Tree 105
"Stirling," A Good-bye Poem for Andrew and Hugh 106
Sands 106
The Wheelchair 107
There Is Just No Way 108
Hi There! 108
The Bus 109
Shoehorn 111
The Babe 112
Lace Doilies 113
Vt. 113
Sophie My Friend 114
? 116
Slime-O 116
The Steeplejack 117
Frank's Obsession 122
Suzy Freeman's Quilts 124
The Walking Guy 125
Forest Bugs 126
SweetieDearyHoneyDarlin' 127

252

*T*hey found him, bedraggled and worn
On a highway, all ragged and torn
They brought him back home
Where he could safe roam
Protected and fed morn to morn.

He lived with them twenty-six years
His rescuers, his overseers.
They gave him good food
Which he sniffed and then chewed
Such as apples and old boutonnieres.

He dozed in the sun all day long
Even dining on scuppernong
The family adored him
So pleased to afford him
Their dear love always and agelong.

He never could really forget
That highway where death he near met.
Had it not been for them
On that fateful AM
He'd've been a roadkill banquet.

He wanted to show them his love
But couldn't. It was unheard of.
His species could not
But he never forgot
Now his life was Valhalla above.

They never could think of a name
And as the years passed it became
A family joke
'Cause they couldn't evoke
A dub for this creature they'd tamed.

Eventually the family knew
They'd name him with no more ado.
For that highway he was named
And that's how he became
The tortoise named Two Fifty Two.

SCARED OR AFRAID??

*A*re there birds afraid of heights?
Some little boys afraid of kites?
Are their cats afraid of mice?
Any gamblers scared of dice?
Are some ice creams afraid of cones?
Are some front porches scared of homes?
Are some minnows scared of brooks?
Some librarians frightened by books?
Are there flowers scared of bees?
Bermuda shorts afraid of knees?
Are there horses scared of saddles?
Any canoes afraid of paddles?
Are there dogs afraid of bones?
Can any teens be scared of phones?
Are there trucks afraid of highways?
Or planes, are some afraid of skyways?
You think some turtles fear the sun?
Are some roadrunners scared to run?
Are any bears afraid of honey?
Are bank accounts afraid of money?
Will whipped cream shudder at strawberries?

Are sea captains scared of ferries?
Are beer drinkers scared of hops?
Any sailors scared of knots?
Are there trees afraid of leaves?
You think shirts are scared of sleeves?
Could there be stars that fear the night?
Could any flashlights fear the light?
Can tires be afraid of roads?
Are summer mushrooms scared of toads?
Are there golf clubs scared of putts?
Do hermits feel afraid of huts?
I guess you think this cannot be,
But I'll confess that as for me
I am afraid of poetry.

CLAY

I wish I had a huge vessel of wondrous, enchanted clay
That I could mold into magical things every single day.
Like building a world where people never resorted to fray
Where kids were never hungry and could always safely
    play.
I'd take great clumps of clay in my hands and make a
    cabaret
Where folks could come to see great shows and never
    have to pay.
I'd build immense museums in poor places with my clay
For people to see the splendor of painters like Monet
And Vincent van Gogh, and Henri Rousseau, Moses,
    Wyeth and Klee.
And then I'd take my special clay and figure out a way
To build a vast coliseum where folks could hear people
    play
The music of all the masters, like Brahms and Bizet, and
    they

Could sit and listen to Pavarotti, Fitzgerald, and Tormé
And Porter, the Gershwins, Berlin, heck, even Doris Day!
And watch wonderful dancers pirouette in graceful ballet,
And hear the sweet poetry of Edna St. Vincent Millet.
And watch spellbinding movies, and cinema vérité,
And schmooze in cafés with roués while sipping mocha
    latte.
I'd then take scoops of my mud and I'd be so proud to say
I'd shape it to all bad diseases, and then without delay
I'd hammer them all to dust, so they could no longer slay
Anyone else in all the world, for forever and a day.
I'd work to make less solemn stuff too, like fudge and
    great horseplay
And circuses, festivals, picnics, and raspberry glacé.
I'd mold the weather of the world so it never rained by day
But just at night like in Camelot; and on each holiday
I'd carve the clay to family scenes of love and mirth and
    glae
Where kids could grow and thrive and live and never
    have to say
"My mother likes to call herself a happy divorcée."
I'd spend a lot of hours carving nature with my clay
Flowers, birds, all animals, a fabulous array.
And all would live in health and peace in the world made
    with my clay
Where every single person would eat like a gourmet.
And no one would ever aspire to be a popinjay.
And I would carve for everyone his very own sobriquet
So everyone would be unique and not just a cliché.
Where everyone could chose to live in their very own
    forté.
Where life is always new and fresh and fine and sweet
    and gay.
And all of us would always be in the core of our heyday.
I'd remodel the world to look like a park in wondrous
    Marseilles

And all men would have broad shoulders, all women
 sweet décolleté.
No bullies would hurt children, and I'd work to find a way
For my clay to keep creatures safe; then I'd get under way
And start to build a warless world although some would
 inveigh
Against all this, for some love war, but to those fools I say
"You call it 'Dreams,' can't happen, but don't let it fade
 away
"Who knows? It could all transpire. It's really not so fey
"For all of us to hope, to dream, to plan, to wish and pray
"That we each could work to make our world a perfect
 place to stay."
I confess I frequently dream in both the night and the day
Of taking that mud and remolding our world in a very
 positive way
With that vessel of clay, with my mystical clay, my
 enchanted, magical clay.

CIRCLES WITHIN CIRCLES WITHIN...

*E*ver notice that life is circles
and we constantly go round and round?
Doubt it? Well think! You'll see it's quite clear
we're like a tail chasing its hound!
   Take laundry, a perfect example;
We wear clothes, and when they show soil,
we haul them to the washing machine,
then circle them back. See? A coil!
   Same with the dishes, am I not right?
We first pull them out of the chest
and dine from them, making them grubby,
then wash them and put them to rest.
   We live day-to-day in our circles
starting off in our warm comfy bunk.

We rise, shower, eat, go to work,
then head back to bed with a plunk.
      Vacations make a very good case
for showing life's just a big hoop.
We pack and leave, have fun in the sun
then return, completing the loop.
      And think how we start out as babies,
we whine, make demands, and are needy.
And when we grow old, we revert,
and whine and demand, and get greedy.
      Money's one thing that we wish
would circle around and return,
but it never does, it goes out in a line
so we circle back and re-earn.
      One circle we all hope won't happen,
the one which we all would elude,
is the circle that gets completed
when our kids return home with their brood.
      Circles are good things in general
like the arms of a mother or dad
when they're wrapped tight 'round scared children
on the nights when the thunder is bad.
      And circles are good when we're chatting
and find we've been too talkative,
then realizing our very bad manners
circle back and say "Oh! Please forgive!"
      Circles have meaning, they're notable
for the times that they're given away.
Made of silver or gold we give them
to our darlings on our wedding day.
      Everyone knows how seeds circle
beginning at first in the earth;
They grow into trees which shake down their seeds
and those new ones then start the rebirth.
      S. Freud had his own circle theories
and said "from the time we're begat

we urgently wish to return to the womb."
Well, I'm not so sure about that.

Old Chris Columbus shouted aloud,
"You fools, the world isn't flat!
"It's round like a ball and I'll prove it."
He sailed off and then circled back.

It's sad but it's often quite true
that we end our lives where we began.
I speak of the hospital here,
where we started, we end our life's span.

Life's ever connecting circles
determine our roundabout fate.
They widen, join, spread and commingle
like rings from stones thrown in a lake.

You see? When you think hard about it,
life's lived by going a-round.
We rush straight ahead and then circle back
like a tail that's chasing its hound.

CLUSTERS

*E*ver noticed how certain things
Like cows and whales and water rings
Cluster together and never part?
You don't have to be awfully smart
To see that stuff just comes together
(I think they plan a get-together.)
No one puts these things up close
It's futile to try to diagnose
Why these things will just gravitate
And sort of natcherly congregate.
Animals, objects, the whole shebangers
But the weirdest clusters of all
Are hangers.

Life Is—

*M*y life is one of gladness
With very little sadness
And rarely any badness.
But sometimes there is madness
Which oft can lead to gadness
And from there to egadness
Which always is forebadness
By both my Mom and Dadness
'Cause they dislike jub'ladness
They say it makes me rashness.
And they get hopping madness
At having to keep tabness
On my grand gift of gabness
And my endless confabness
With every lass and ladness
Who'll listen to my blabness.
They tell me I should gab less
But that I just won't address
'Cause I refuse to chat less!
But let's do some more chatness
About life's likely drabness.
Say, it's not iron-cladness
That life should be all gladness.
There really can be drabness
And badness, sadness, madness.
I know. I've seen it happ'ness.
But joy? You've got to grabness
And on your own behalfness
So you won't just go daftness
At all the world's sad crapness.
Life really can be fabless
And it need not be hapless
Get right in it smack-dabness
And cram your life with joy!

CRICKETS

*T*wo things I'd like to know
About crickets and their ways
So here they are, and oh
They'll vex me all my days.
The first you know you've tried
(But the bug's outwitted you)
In cities or countryside
Here's exactly what you do;
When you hear one in the bush
Calling strong and loud and clear
The cricket'll instantly shoosh
When you try to make it appear.
Now, I know crickets are loved
That they're thought to bring one luck
(So I'd never want them shoved
Beneath the wheels of a truck.)
The second thing which annoys
Me about that raucous fiend
Is that endless, chirping noise
Which keeps me up, like caffeine.
I wish at night they'd snooze
And stop that bleepity-bleep
Chirping. It does not amuse.
Can't they just sleepity-sleep?

BRUSSELS SPROUTS ETC.

*W*hat are the names of the louts
Who invented Brussels sprouts?
Are they the very same guys
Who invented spinach pies?
Is the person still alive
Who told us we should like endive?

Tell me, what's with rutabagas?
They're not even fit for beggars.
Do you like to eat good treats?
Be sure to stay away from beets.
What about that ghastly liver?
The very thought just makes me shiver.
Do you like to eat raw oysters?
I would rather live in cloisters.
What's the deal with corn meal mush?
Who can eat that hideous squush?
And certain people's foul meatloaf
Looks and tastes just like peatloaf.
Say, whoever thought that squid
Was anything more than just viscid?
And that hummus. Who likes that?
It tastes a lot like roadkill rat.
Oh yes, and then that gross tahini
Snubbed by even by piggies guinea.
And what on earth's the deal with veal?
It's meat, I guess, but it's not real.
I sometimes take a look at fish
And would much rather eat the dish.
And how about that herbal tea?
Like used boiled socks it tastes to me.
Some folks like those shoo fly pies.
I think they're really baked with flies.
I'd really like to jail the fellow
Who created mango jello.
Black licorice you say you'd scarf?
Oh I beg, don't make me barf.
And let me talk, please, with the fiend
Who thought up that nouvelle cuisine.
Have you ever dined on ramps?
Don't try them. They will give you cramps.
Now, how about that boiled squirrel?
Oh, no thanks. It makes me hurl.

Veggie paté in aspic?
Truly makes me very sick.
And not even on a dare
Would I ever eat jugged hare.
The very sight of pig's knuckles
Can't inspire me to chuckles.
If you can eat that bad salt herring
You deserve some Croix de guerring.
One of the very worst foods ever
Is haggis, swear to me you'll never.
Armadillo they say is great
If you love to eat breastplate.
Would I ever eat broiled ass?
No. I'd rather chew ground glass.
Chicory, okra, cukes or kale?
The thought of those things makes me pale.
And from a plate piled with Swiss chard
I would gallop fast backward.
You like whelks? Those gastropods?
Not I! Even in roulades.
Sardines as food is a joke
Even their smell makes me choke.
Some countries view as a prize
A main course featuring sheep's eyes.
I know I hate a lot of food
And ought to show more gratitude.
You want to know which one's the worst?
I shall tell, before you burst.
I mostly hate those heinous louts
The guys who invented Brussels sprouts.
They're the worst of all I hate
On that I won't equivocate.

ME AND MY CICADAS

*T*he loveliest sound in the summer to me
Along with the birds' sweet tweedle-dee-dee
Is the sound of the large homopterous bug
Found in all nature, (sometimes in vug.)
Cicadas! Cicadas! My favorite thing
In the summer, hot summer when they sing!
Cicadas! Cicadas! I do love that creatcha
There's so much about them I'd like to teachya;
They belong to the family cicadidae
(That's Latin for that kind of insect, they say.)
Yes, they're cicadas, and I will relate
I could listen to them any time, any date.
The noise of this bug makes me celebrate summer
Though I've never seen one, they're there by the number.
I love their loud call, and I would like to see one
But I'll settle for hearing if I can't screen one.
I don't mean to sound like an epicure
On these bugs that take seventeen years to mature
Who like to emit a resonant shrill
That can only be likened to escadrille
Which they make by shaking some belly membranes
(This doesn't require bug legerdemain.)
To us it's just simply inconceivable
And actually, plainly quite unbelievable,
That cicadas make that glorious drone
Like humming on cellophane over a comb.
I cherish that sound, and my eager ears
Have so loved to hear it over the years.
In the summers, the sound makes me stop and smile
And even go out in the sun for a while.
But though I dearly cherish their din,
Though my love for those bugs makes some folks grin,
There's one thing about 'em that's been a bothah
Should we say sik-AID-uh or should we say sik-AHD-uh??

BUT NOT IN THE BACK YARD

*I*t's such a dear, sweet thing to do
Keeping the old folks close to you.
Now, I don't mean while they're on earth
But when they're gone, for what it's worth.
I see it happen all the time;
After the old folks start their climb
Heavenward, the heirs make plans
(After checking with family clans)
To bury the old folks in their yard.
What could show a higher regard
Than to hail them every day
From the windows, May through May.
And so they do it and it's fine
That Mom and Dad are 'neath the pine
Or over yon in the south forty
Buried near Uncle Bill, and "Shorty"
Their little dog who passed last year
Along with their feline, "Catty Dear."
Now this is all just fine and good
And shows great love, as well it should.
But pray, what does the family do
When it finds it has to move?
What about dear Mom and Dad?
The brand-new owners won't be glad
To take on this grave obligation
Of your dead folks' bright salvation.
I can't think who'd want that job
From poorest slob to richest nabob.
It's not the brand-new owner's duty
To take on this unwanted booty.
So when your dear ones you must bury
Haul them to the cemetery.

'BYE BILL

*H*ere's a tale 'bout a butterfly named Bill
Who happ'ly lived on a flower covered hill.
He had all the nectar he could ever need.
And he'd spend all day long fluttering the glebe.
Bill's very best friend was a huge toad named Harry
But in spite of his bigness, Harry was chary.
He was too scared to leave the flowered hill
And wanted never to leave his friend Bill.
But shy Harry yearned a more varied cuisine
He wanted rare bugs, on this hill thus unseen.
He was hungry, he said, and wanted to try
New bugs in new places, dragon and deerfly.
But Bill just laughed
   and said "Harry my
   friend,
"You're just much too
   wimpy. Sorry to
   offend,
"But you'll never be
   able to leave this big
   hill
"Or to even leave me,
   your old friend. Me! Bill!"
Then Bill turned his back and laughed very loud,
And shy Harry shed tears and kept his head bowed.
Bill shouldn't have mocked and hurt Harry, his friend
And for the poor toad, this was simply the end.
Bill, sad to say, forgot Harry's swift tongue,
Too late! ZOTT! Bill the butterfly was done.

IBID WHO?

*W*ho is this guy Ibid?
He really wrote a lot.
Ibid was proliffid
He was a true zealot.
But I've done some research
On Ibid's giant yield.
And so I must besmirch
His name. The man concealed
The fact that he stole words
From other author's toils.
And I have also heard
He took those verbal spoils
And claimed they were his own.
He was very liable
To steal from any source
Even from the Bible!
Now isn't that the worst?
He also claims he writ
Stuff Shakespeare really wrote
He was a real nit-wit
And really should be smote
For pinching all those words
And claiming they were his.
He's really got a nerve!
Lay off, Ibid. Gee whiz.

LEARNING

*W*e learn and we learn, every minute we're alive, it's the
    credo we learn to live by.
And we even learn at our very last minute, since it's then
    that we learn how to die.

23

THE BURNED HOUSE

I walked in the woods by myself that day
I wanted to be alone.
The woods were where I was never afraid
The woods for me were home.

The day was so pure, the air meadow-sweet
Joy-tears spilled from my eyes.
The woods were my haven and my retreat
My earthrise, moonrise, sunrise.

I walked up a hill all covered with trees
On an overgrown trail
The sun washed down, there were birds, there were bees
I laughed at a cottontail.

I stopped in a spot and looked all around
The sun was dappled green.
And just as always, I stood there spellbound
And thanked this transcendent scene.

But this sylvan spot was quite new to me
I'd never been there before.
But woods never cause me anxiety
They are my life, my savior, my core.

Something compelled me to turn and to look
Down the small hill to my right.
And there it was at the straggled path's crook
And I cried out at the sight.

I saw the remains of a house that day
It was just a hole in the ground.
The house had burned down, and that was the way
I saw the house that I'd found.

I could still see stairs I was sure had led
To the small kitchen, I knew.
I could still see the shapes of rooms, the shed,
Still outlines left to view.

I clambered over the foundation's walls

And sat where the parlour was
And imagined the family therewithal
Living as each family does.
     I sat in the ashes and looked around
Imagining them all there
I saw them at work and I heard the sound
Of their joy and their despair.
     I looked at (I guessed) where a window had been
And "saw" flowers in the yard
I wondered if those kids played games akin
To my own, those dear to my heart.
     I saw an old cooking pot dented and burnt
And wondered if it had been
Charred in the fire or when the house burned
Down to this awful ruin.
     The remains of a wooden chair stood near
It had rockers, I could see
I know the mother had rocked her babes here
The way my mother rocked me.
     A burned sled and wagon lay in the trees
Left behind by a child
The sight of them brought back sweet memories
I then looked away, and I smiled.
     And in a corner to my great surprise
A small piano stood proud.
The old ivory keys now paralyzed
It's richly carved case burned black and brown.
     But what touched me most was the old chimney
Still standing in spite of all.
Made from great rocks, now scorched, I could see
The fire had not made it fall.
     I wondered then if that family had
Met by its hearth's soft glow
To tell of their day's events, good or bad
There in that bungalow.
     The fire had taken their home away

And left them with nothing more
Than a burned out shell, and nothing to say
Of how it had been before.
Long twisted vines crept through the stone walls
As I sat where life was once.
And I heard soft woods sounds, breezes, birdcalls
And watched two hawks at their hunts.

Had they died in that fire? Were they safe?
Had it happened in the night?
So far off in the woods, had they escaped?
Had help gotten there all right?

The house was not large out there in the woods
But life had lived there one time
I knew there was love and a good likelihood
Of new babies all the time.

I imagined a mother cooking there
Loving, funny and proud.
A cat on the hearth, a big old armchair
From which Dad would read aloud.

I sat in the ashes of that little home
And started to softly weep
Dappled sunlight turned slowly to gloam
I wanted to curl and sleep.

But I stood up in that charred, blackened mess
Then climbed up the burned out walls
The pure twilight sounds were now coalesced
Now clear were the cricket calls.

I walked down that path so covered with brush
And knew that I never should
Again see that place so still in the hush
That little burned house in the wood.

WHITE DREAM

I'd always dreamed when I was a kid
That I'd own a home, oh, so splendid!
Filled to the roof with elegant stuff,
I'd never be able to have enough.
In my dream home there would be one thing
Much more important than anything;
I can't explain this need that I had
I'd always wished it, (it was no fad.)
My wondrous home would not be complete
My elegant digs just couldn't compete
If I didn't have one certain thing
(And this thing could not be just anything,)
But something I've always thought made a home
Just perfect. You see I've always known
That this would turn the lowliest home
Into the very glowiest home
Where I could spend every single day
Surrounded by nothing déclassé.
But back to that thing I insisted I own
In my home, my prized and sumptuous home;
Not chandeliers or platinum fixtures
Not treasure chests with dozens of mixtures
Of jewels and coinage and pieces of eight
Not laces, satins or silks by the crate.
Not buckets of jewels worn by a queen
Nor stacks of gold glowing like Hallowe'en
Not priceless paintings upon my walls
Or oriental rugs spread through my halls
Not crystal, silver, jade or topaz
Or furnishings once owned by Louis Quinze
Or have millions stashed beneath a floorboard
Or keep my precious tiaras stored
In diamond-encrusted gold canisters.
No, my dream home must just have white banisters.

A to Z Color Me

*A*lphabet letters have colors, you know.
You didn't? Well yes, they do.
As many colors as in a rainbow
Puce. Mauve and teal. Even blue.

Let us begin with the first letter, A.
It's yellow, and that's for sure
Oh no, not the yellow of a bright day
But that of a school bus tincture.

B? That's easy. It's the color of blue
Blue like the blue of jeans.
Not blue like the blue in a tattoo
Nor a blue that might have been.

OK, now there's C, and they say this shade,
'Twas loved by Agamemnon.
It is not silver, gold, ruby or jade
C's the tint of the lemon.

D? It's the color of orange, of course
Ain't that what you've always thunk?
If you saw that tint on a pig or horse
You'd prob'ly thunk you were drunk.

E? It's white. It could be no other
I'm not sure why I think that.
It's the white of the feathers of a sea plover
And not the white of a lab rat.

A really dark color belongs to F
A very dark grey indeed.
Although it's gloomy, don't turn an ear deaf
'Cause dull F just wants to succeed.

G, oh gee whiz, it's quite clearly green
But not like gross yucko guts.
G is the color of cool wintergreen
And often like unripe chestnuts.

H is a tough one, but I think it's ice
You know, kind of grey and cold.
Maybe the color of bellies of mice
When they're stuck in the cold in the wold.

Let's see now, there's I. I think I's dark brown
Like pieces of rich, creamy fudge.
But don't ever let letter I make you frown
By thinking it looks like sludge.

Now comes that nice little letter called J
It brings to mind just one hue
I think old J is a lovely pearl grey
A grey with no hint of blue.

Now K is always the color of red
I add here a small caveat
It's like the red of the quilt on my bed.
But don't ever think you'll see that.

L is like rust, and I don't know why
I see that in letter L.
But I do, and you know? I would not lie
(If you lie, you could go to hell.)

M is a nice tint, like robin's egg blue
Without those speckles in it.
Would I like to have my eyes be that hue?
Oh, in a New York minute.

N is quite likely a nice dark maroon
The color of blue mixed with red.
Sometimes bar stools are maroon in saloons
But rarely seen on a biped.

O, oh, my favorite, the color of cream!
The kind you see on a farm.
Or maybe O's shade is like a moonbeam
Old O has a great deal of charm.

P is like indigo, really quite nice
The color P looks like that.
Yep, like indigo, I'll say twice.
So that's the deal now, thereat.

Q is an odd one. I think it's aqua.
Q isn't used a real lot.
If you like that shade, I sure won't knock ya
And would not start a boycott.

R is like melon, the kind with black seeds
"Water," they call it I think.
Rosy and cool, it goes great with meads.
It's color is twixt red and pink.

I think letter S is like apricot
A lovely orangey-gold
It's got pretty curves, I love S a lot
S is a sight to behold.

T, now that's tough, but I think it's loyal
To purple. Do you think so?
I mean that worn by a Windsor Royal
Or maybe folks in Morocco.

Frequently U's comes right after Q's
So it has to harmonize
With aqua, remember? What, did you snooze?
U then could only be byje.

I think V has the pigment of curry
The stuff in Indian fare
(Now don't ever eat curry hurried,
Or you'll feel your throat pipes stripped bare.)

I think W is like cranberry
Which they say is good for you.
Thanksgiving is when it's most very
Used with much hullabaloo.

X is a letter often ignored
But I see color in it.
OK, here it is! Prepare to be floored!
It's chartreuse, I'd like to submit.

Y's got its very own color. Why not?
It's pink. You don't need a jury.
Pink! Like the eye of the cranky rhinop
As it charges you in a fury.

And Z, final Z. I think it's quite black
Like Zoro's cape or moustache.
Now Zoro, they tell us, was a real quack
But he had a certain panache.

So you see? All letters can conjure up
One color, or two or three.
Colors of mud, or even turnup
Well, that's how it seems to me.

FIRE AND WHAT?

I know this sounds terribly opprobrious,
But I've always been dreadfully curious
About the fright'ning and often hurled threat
Of "Fire and Brimstone" stuff that you get
Raining down while you peacefully doze
In church where you'd never, ever suppose
That the preacher is preaching straight at you
While you gently snooze, not having a clue
That this fire and brimstone stuff is nigh
And that he's quite sure the second you die
You'll be dipped straight into it and won't get
Out 'til eternity ends, he would bet.
He may be right, but oh, hell's bells!
Must they always shout about death knells?
Tell me please, if you so desire. And
Can one say "brimstone" without saying "fire and?"
But back to the main point of this essay;
Could someone please define for me today
In fact what the meaning of "brimstone" is?
Could Native Americans like Shoshones
Tell us where we could find this rare rock?
Or maybe a shrink who's studied Rorschach
Can tell us how this weird, scary stuff
Affects Ids and Egos? But off the cuff
I finally thought I'd get the real dope
And look up the word, or write to the Pope
To 'splain what it is; a stone on the brim
Of a crater? Or did the Seraphim
Lie on it, hoping six digits to tan
So they'd look healthy in the Vatican
Or while hov'ring over some frightened souls
Who know they're the sinners for whom the bell tolls?
But no, no, it's nothing at all like that
(Although it really should not be sneered at.)

Brimstone's just sulphur, subject to fire
So I'd suggest, before you expire
To mend your mean ways, repent and all that
So you won't have to swim in all that hot fat
Of hell, or wherever that preacher says
You'll go where you'll find yourself in a real mess,
Where non-quenching fire will start at your legs
But worse, you'll breathe in the stench of bad eggs.

BE GREAT

*W*ouldn't it be great
To sleep in the sunshine without getting burned?
Wouldn't it be great
To have tons of money without its being earned?
Wouldn't it be great
To eat pots of chocolate without getting zits?
Wouldn't it be great
If we could go through life and never deal with twits?
Wouldn't it be great
If poppyseeds would never stick in our teeth?
Wouldn't it be great
If our slaved-over lawns didn't resemble a heath?
Wouldn't it be great
To make love in a meadow and not get caught?
Wouldn't it be great
If they planned a great war and nobody fought?
Wouldn't it be great
If we could stay skinny and never feel hunger?
Wouldn't it be great
When we looked in the mirror we saw someone younger?
Wouldn't it be great
If we never got an itch in a place we oughtn't?
Wouldn't it be great
If certain people weren't always unthoughtn't?

Wouldn't it be great
If employees always washed before leaving rest rooms?
Wouldn't it be great
If the best beds at home weren't just in the guestrooms?
Wouldn't it be great
If realtors, car and insurance people told the truth?
Wouldn't it be great
If we could still use that great old word "forsooth?"
Wouldn't it be great
If the dishwasher and dryer were always empty?
Wouldn't it be great
If teens would stop acting so endlessly contempty?
Wouldn't it be great
If someone could logically explain geometry?
Wouldn't it be great
If certain tardy friends learned about chronometry?
Wouldn't it be great
If Hitler and Stalin and Genghis died at birth?
Wouldn't it be great
If the doctor would stop haranguing about our girth?
Wouldn't it be great
If our new, cute, sweet puppies never pooped?
Wouldn't it be great
If we could always watch Betty while she booped?
Wouldn't it be great
If people who said "I love you" never pretended?
Wouldn't it be great
If I finally got this long poem ended?

ANYMORE

*T*here are many sad words we've heard heretofore
But the saddest for me is "anymore."
A word which was never meant to be sad
A word which was never meant to be bad.
But for me, it's sorrowful; I'll tell you why
(Well, not so sorrowful as to make me cry.)
Oh maybe sometimes, but that is because
The words which come first cause heart windlestraws.
Here are some samples of just what I mean
(You will understand, once I set the scene;)

"I'm not able to do that...anymore."
"I'm not permitted to drive...anymore."
"We cannot have a dog...anymore."
"I cannot read my books...anymore."
"I cannot hear my music...anymore."
"I cannot ever eat that...anymore."
"I cannot take those trips...anymore."

The list is quite long, as you can see
But this should explain why it must be
That this is the saddest term I've heard
The most melancholy of any word.
"I can't run and sing in the woods...anymore."
"I cannot eat chocolate...any more."
"We can't stay married...anymore."
"He's died. He's not with me...anymore."
"Our children don't live here...anymore."

My eyes are now filled with hot tears which will pour
Down my cheeks since these words make me awfully
heartsore.
So you see, I must stop. I can't write...anymore.

THE BERRY BOY

I saw this kid asleep at the switch
Next to his car, parked in a ditch.
The back was open and this young male
Had a sign in his lap, "Strawberries 4 Sale."
I needed some berries but had not the heart
To awaken this lad to sell me a quart.
His mouth hung open and I very much feared
His young tongue would soon be sorely sun-seared.
But I did not wish to wake the young guy
And so I drove off with an eye to the sky.
I saw some dark clouds gather up there
And thought "Oh good, now I won't have to care.
"Because that boy will now sleep in shade
"His tongue won't burn, my fears are allayed."
After some hours I found I was done
And began to make my home return run.
"Maybe," I thought, "that boy's now awake
"And I can buy berries to put in my cake!"
I got in my car. It started to rain
My lovely warm day then started to wane.
I could hardly see, the rain was so thick
The windshield was fogged, the roads were quite slick.
The boy was still there, next to his car
It looked like he'd sold not one berry thus far.
He sat there asleep, the sign in his lap
He seemed to be taking the very same nap.
His clothing was drenched, his hair was too
Of his being soaked, he had not one clue.
His mouth still hung open I saw with a frown,
Well, his tongue wouldn't burn; now I feared he would
  drown.

THE BANANA

*I*t was back in aught nine
She was just twenty five
A young mother of four
They were really quite poor.
Each day was a struggle
To keep away trouble
And as much as able
Keep food on the table.
One notable day
In the sweet month of May
In walked her dear man
With a gift in his hand.

"What is that?" she cried
(His grin was so wide!)
"A banana," he said
She just shook her head.
"I've read about them,"
She said, and said then
"How will we eat it?
"You think I should beat it
"Into eggs or a cake?
"Or pray, should I bake
"It in a large pan
"And serve it with jam?"
The family pondered
And solemnly wondered
And then just went mute
'Bout this strange yellow fruit.
The wife could have peeled it
Or in a crock sealed it.
She thought "Should I broil it?
"Oh no, I'll just boil it."
So she did 'zactly that
And you know what hap'd.

THE STORY OF DOC AND KAY

Once upon a time there was a man with a name
No one had heard much; not many could claim.
The name was "Einar," he was called as a boy
(That name wasn't found much in the hoi polloi!)
When Einar grew up and chose his profession
He knew now at last, at his own discretion
He'd change that name to something more fittin'
Something more easily said and yes, written.
In his proud new profession, he was (take note,)
Brilliant at debugging the Ear, Nose and Throat.
Yes now he was a doctor, solid as rock
And now he could change his odd name to just "Doc."
Doc was a good man and great at his job
A gifted physician, virtuoso with swab.
He married, had children and did it again
Continued his practice, retired and then
Decided he'd aged a bit more than he'd planned
So, alone now, decided to take things in hand
And move to a place he'd heard much about.
He sold all his stuff, packed up and moved out
To Elizabethtown, to a special place;
The Masonic Home, a wondrous, vast space
Of beauty and flowers, orchards and lands
Of splendid buildings built by many hands
Belonging to Masons. (Doc's one but won't gloat,
'Bout that or 'bout being Dr. Ear, Nose and Throat!)
And so Doc moved in there in 2/ ninety four
And happily lived in Masonic splendor.
But Doc was lonely, and he often thought
He'd like to meet someone, but knew it was naught
To be. Although women were everywhere there,
None caught his fancy, none devil-may-care
Enough to attract him, to make him fall hard

And so he lived nicely, but kept up his guard.
And then one fine day in 2/ ninety-seven
He looked up and saw a sweet piece of heaven.
A lady was standing there. Her name was Kay.
(Her real name was Kathryn.) She was like a ray
Of sudden sunshine. He loved her blue eyes.
It was love at first sight. His heart just capsized.
Kay looked at him and she felt the same
As he did, she loved him, her heart was aflame.
Kay told Doc she'd worked at NJ Bell many years
Then retired to follow other careers.
She happily moved to Elizabethtown
To the Masonic Home, that place of renown.
Kay herself had been married before
But now was alone, like Doc. Furthermore
She was the same age as this man. What a dream!
She knew right away they'd make quite a team.
They liked the same music, big bands and such
They liked lots of things the same and much
More! Like seafood and chocolate butter creams
This couple discovered they shared the same dreams.
But back to the music, their favorite tunes
Were mostly about love and spooning and moons.
Kay loved "Always," and discovered her pal
Doc loved the song "For Me and My Gal."
        "I'll be loving you, always,
        "With a love that's true, always.
        "When the things you've planned
        "Need a helping hand
            "I will understand, always...always,"
Kay sang to her Doc with her heart.
                "The bells are ringing
                "For me and my gal,"
        "The birds are singing, for me and my gal
        "Everybody's been knowin'
        "To a wedding we're goin'

"And for weeks they've been sewin'
"Every Suzie and Sal,"
Doc sang to his Kay with his heart.
So they got engaged, but not for too long
For at this stage of life, it is evensong.
Kay and her Doc, not quite centenarians
Are happy and youthful octogenarians.
So in three short months, they would sign on the page
Their married names! At eighty-one years of age!
Plans were then made for a wonderful wedding
At the Masonic Home in that splendid setting
The place where they first saw each other and met
For the first time, and they will never forget
The love that they felt, right in a twinkling!
Neither had ever had the least inkling
That they would meet, not in Paris or Rome
But in Pennsylvania at the Masonic home!
So the people all gathered in month eleven
The sixth day it was, the year ninety seven.
On that glory day the Mason named Doc
Joined his dear Kay in holy wedlock
The world wishes decades of joy to this pair
And their late-in-life love they so sweetly share.

ANN WAS A FOOL

*I*t was awful for Ann when she saw all that blood on that
    terrible, scary day
But calling a doctor would shame her she said, then said
    "It'll all go away."
Ann wept and she screamed, and prayed awfully hard,
    and frequently lost her breath.
She did not call the doctor, so soon after that, Ann was
    embarrassed to death.

WYETH AND DOT

"Oh no," I said, "No! Not I!
"It'd be so tacky!" cried I.
"He is the artist I've sighed for
"And he's the one I would die for
"If he asked me, but he'd never.
("Tho I'd do it.) But to endeavor
"To collect his autograph?
"Oh, I couldn't. What a gaffe!"
"Ah, come on," said my friend Dot.
"Do it! Do it! Take a shot!"
"Oh no!" I whined, "He'll turn me down!"
I pouted hard and forced a frown.
"Me? Ask Mr. Andrew Wyeth?
"Oh my no! I'd rather dyeth!
"Besides, see? The man is eating
"Lunch over there, with his sweeting."
"You're a fool," said my friend Dot
"No," said I, "I'm really not.
"I just would never dream to ask
"A dining man to do that task."
"OK," said Dot, my dearest friend
"But you'll be sorry in the end."
And so she did it! Yes! She did!
While I squirmed, mumbling "God forbid!"
Straight to Mr. Wyeth's table
Marched my friend, cool and able!
While I jealously stood and watched
Thinking, "Oh dear, now she's botched
"That great artist's private lunch."
But he looked just as pleased as punch!
Andrew gladly gave to Dot
His autograph, and then she got
Helga's too, since she was there.

(Remember her? She was bare
In many paintings done of her
By Andrew Wyeth, oh yessir!)
One hundred and twenty something
Paintings of his favorite dumpling
Helga. She was eating too
And signed without e'en one to-do.
('Drew'd also painted Helga dressed
And Helga dressed was maybe best.
But in each stage of dishabille
Andrew made her look so real.)
Like all of us they've aged a bit
They're wrinkled now, and not so fit.
Helga'd fill the canvas more now
And Andrew's face is kind of scored now.
But Wyeth's paintings do still touch
All hearts. The man has given much.
And Helga, was she his paramour?
No one ever knew for sure.
And there she sat having lunch
With Andrew Wyeth. Or was it brunch?
Doesn't matter, Dot got both
Signatures. I took an oath
To never again be such a wimp
(Or maybe I should say a "simp.")
To make it worse, Wyeth said
to Dot, "Well yes, please go ahead
"And hand your pen and paper here
"And we shall sign it now, my dear.
"Normally I would just say 'no,'
"But this one time I will forgo
"My usual habit; you see
"I admire your bravery!
"So here's my name, with delight!"
And then the artist took a bite
Of his lunch, but then he quite

Grasped Dot's hand and held it tight!
And I felt like a troglodyte
For passing up the only chance
I'll ever have to get a glance
Of Andrew Wyeth's signing well
His great name with his pointelle
To a paper offered him
By me. But no, I was too dim
To take a chance such as that
The way my friend Dot did, the brat.
(And by the way, when he signed,
Dot's pen and paper were really MINE!
But oh, the hand that squeezed dear Dot's
Had painted great works by the lots.)
But I then did the next best thing
And found his car, and with shaking
Hands I wrote the man a note
I'd always wished to, and I quote;
"I've waited nearly all my life
"To have the chance I take to write
"These words, dear man; I thank you so
"For allowing lowly me to know
"Your heavenly works in prints and books,
"On museum's walls and hung in nooks."
And then I signed my very name
And fantasized he'd do the same
And write to me and thank me for
The note I left in his car door.
He read my note and drove away
With Helga at the wheel that day
And as they passed I shouted "Thanks!"
And Wyeth waved but looked quite blank.
I looked at Dot and said "Ah ha!
"See? To me he waved 'Ta Ta!'
"You, you got his autograph
"But me, he tried to telegraph

"His thanks to me for my sweet note."
And Dot said, "You are such a dolt!"
And then we knew we should depart
But first two stones from where he'd parked
I got, and gave her one. (Tee hee,
I kept the biggest one for me!)

IMBIBING

$\mathcal{T}$hey look at me as if I'm one step lower than a common
pooper scooper
Because I don't drink! Booze that is, and that makes me a
    bourgeois party pooper.
I wish I could drink, but I can't because the taste of
    hootch is just repellent
Although everyone denies this and says well, "Well-aged
    brandy tastes excellent."
I maintain the taste is like rotted socks worn for a year by
    a swamp dweller.
And ancient Scotches? Yucko. That stuff tastes like scrap-
    ings from a caveman's cellar.
And what's the great big deal about getting drunk? How
    can that possibly feel good?
Drooling, barfing, saying and doing things we'd erase the
    next day if we could.
And what's so great about looking and feeling like skunk
    roadkill the next morning?
Really, they should print on the bottle what you'll feel
    like, give you a fair warning.
Sometimes I think "oh dear, everyone is having such fun
    here, and I'm so bored,"
As the party surges, and soused people carouse, drinking
    all they can absorb.
They're laughing and dancing and working that old cliche
    of lampshades on their heads

While I'm wandering around upstairs and looking longing-
   ly at my host's beds.
Now I have always heard it's a heavenly thing to drink a
   very fine wine
With truly wonderful meals and all the trimmings. (I
   heard it on the grapevine.)
I've tried it several times with a highly recommended,
   expensive brew
But even though the wine's quite costly, it still tastes like
   the water in the loo.
And after about half a glass, it all just turns to vinegar on
   my tongue
So it's wasted on me, just wasted, and the next morning,
   my tongue tastes like dung.
And another thing that happens to me when I have a sip
   or two of booze
Is that I laugh and laugh and get really loud, all before I
   puke on my shoes.
So again I have to ask, what on earth is the big deal?
   What is all the fuss?
Booze is bad for you, wrecks your brain and can turn you
   into the size of a bus.
So for me, my very dear boozing friends, hootch just
   doesn't have absolute use
The taste is gross, I hate what it does to me, so I guess I'll
   stick with fruit juice.

EVEN THEN STUFF CAUGHT IN TEETH WAS GROSS

I'll bet it used to always happen even to the mighty god
   Bacchus
That when he ate poppy seeds or bean sprouts his teeth
   looked like an abacus.

ELEPHANTS

*I*n early October we got in the car
We pointed it north, and we planned to go far.
Fall leaves on the trees nearly blinded our eye
Sweet'ning our hearts, making us sigh.
Orange and yellow, chartreuse, and red
I had to make comment, and so I said
"Are we lucky or what, to live where we do,
To see all this splendor as if it were new?"
He said "yes my sweet, we are more than blessed."
We laughed at the dazzle, our fingers caressed.
More Northward we sped, watching ducks in their V's,
Trav'lling high searching islands in warm south seas.
Then pick-ups drove by and I saw with dismay
Fine moose strapped to truck beds; they'd died on that
      day.
"Must hunters do that?" I asked of my honey.
"They've got kids to feed, and don't have much money."
"Oh, OK," I said, but averted my eye
The next time I saw a dead moose passing by.
We kept driving Northward, the view got more fair
We laughed as we travelled, we had not a care.
Quite often we stopped to stare at the views
And watched deer line up at a stream by the twos.
He would not believe me when I shouted out
"Stop! I see elephants lying about!"
"Yeah, right," said my love as he put on the speed
"Your fancy works o'ertime! Elephants indeed!"
"I'm really not kidding," I cried out to him,
He turned up the music to cover my din.
"Turn 'round this instant!" I was now screaming.
"No way!" he roared back, "You know you're just dream-
      ing."
"Am not," I yelled loudly, "and you're a big jerk."
"Are too," he said back, "And you're going berserk."

But he stopped nonetheless and turned the car 'round
And drove to the spot, and made not a sound.
How haughty I felt when he saw what I'd seen,
As he sat in the car, his stare sharp and keen.
Yes, there lying lazy, all hot in
    the sun
Was a herd of el'phants, each
    more than a ton.
Their owner snoozed
    close, and he snored
    just a bit,
While all we could do
    was just stare there
    and sit.
A diner was near, a small
    car and some shacks
And some birds pecked
    gently at the beasts'
    backs.
"Why are they here?" my
    man asked with awe.
"Got me," I said smugly.
    "But I knew what I saw."

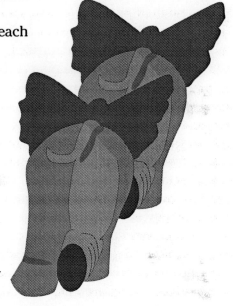

"Now don't get self-righteous. It does not become you."
"Well, you never believe me, even though some do."
"I'll try to do better, to always believe you,
"E'en when you see el'phants. I do hate to peeve you."
"OK then," I said, "Well, let's get on our way."
"What? You don't want to know what that guy has to say?
"Why he's got elephants sleeping on dirt?
"Well, all right," I said, deliberately curt.
"Tut tut," said my man, and we opened the doors
And walked toward the guy in the midst of his snores.
We tapped him gently, but he woke with a start
And we were afraid we'd startled his heart.
"Forgive us," we said, "but we wanted to know

"Why you have el'phants here, high and low."
The man rubbed his eyes, glanced 'round with a frown,
Looked up at us, groaned, then he looked down.
"I sometimes get drunk," he said and he sighed.
"And I wander around, woe is me!" he cried.
He held his head tightly, arms propped on his knees,
"I snook into the circus last night. Oh jeez."
"Oh no," we both chorused. "What then did you do?"
"I let loose these el'phants. Oh no! Boo hoo!"
"Now don't get excited," we said calmingly,
But the man bowed his head and wept sobbingly.
"I guess that they liked me," he wailed and he groaned,
"And so they decided to follow me home."
"We'll call the police! We have a car phone."
"Oh please don't do that!" the man said with a moan.
"They'll put me in jail, I know for a fact,
"They've jailed me before, and that is that."
"OK," we said, "but we just cannot leave you."
"I'll be fine," said the man. "Sorry to grieve you."
Reluctant we were when it came time to go,
But he reassured us, said "My name is Joe."
"Well so long, Joe, we sure wish you well."
"Don't worry," he said, "You never can tell,
"They may follow me back to the tents. I'll just hope!
"Whenever I drink, I sure act like a dope,
"I'll stop as of now. It only brings trouble,
"Bringing me sorrow, and then I see double.
"Because of the booze, I'm now stuck with these beasts
"I've got to return them, to do that at least."
We drove off and waved, and I said to my love,
"Believe me next time?" He said "Yes, my dove.
"I'll believe you always, e'en when you say
"You see el'phants or elves. I'll know you're not fey."
"Then I guess you'll believe me," I said with a smile.
"We truly passed Elvis back there 'bout a mile!"

What's In a Name? What's Not?

*Y*ou ask "what's in a name?"
Well I can tell you what.
Just everything I claim,
It matters lots, ah but

We never stop to think
How harmful it can be
To name our babies "Dink,"
Or "Chick" or "Moon" or "Three."

I knew a kid named "Three,"
He really hated that
His folks could not agree
On naming their begat.

He was their dear third child,
But they could not accede
On how to have him filed
And so they filed him "Three."

Three found this very grim,
And tried to be a scout
But wished they'd named him Tim,
Instead of an amount.

I have a name I hate
It's "Elsie." I'll avow
It never feels so great
Being likened to that cow.

The Borden Company
decided to present
a mascot named Elsie.
I'd love to meet the gent

Who thought this ad campaign
Would sell milk by the ton.
I wish he had refrained
And never had begun

To tout that weird bovine
To name her with a name
That really just was mine
Yeah, he's the guy I blame

For all the fifth grade boys
Tormenting me each day
With comments they enjoyed
Like "You make curds and whey?

"Please pull your apron high
Let's see those udders hang."
I wanted just to die
It was an endless pang.

Those vicious little creeps
Made school a horrid thing
Their words cut way down deep
And had an awful sting.

But things like that will pass
And then the boys moved on
To tease another lass
Whose name, alas, was Fawn.

But oddly, and somehow
I missed the songs they'd do
Like "Elsie The Borden Cow"
Followed by "Moooo Moooo."

One day I changed my name
To letters L and C
It really was the same
But it felt good to me.

I'm older now, and gee,
I could go back again
To Elsie, not LC
But oh, I think "But then,

"Perhaps I'll meet a guy
"Who'll think it's quite a joke
"And think he's awfully wry
"By starting into poke

"Great fun about my name."
And then I'll get aloof
And cause him to be lame
By kicks from my back hoof.

So think before you rule
On what you name your kid
Think how they'll survive school
I know, because I did.

What's in a name you say?
A lot, I promise that.
Just sympathize, OK?
Name gently your dear brat.

YUM

I've always wondered if bugs, for
    lunch,
Only seek bugs to eat who crunch.

EMMA

I know a huge dog named Emma
Who poses an awful dilemma.
Emma's dilemma's her tail
Which when wagged is a hurricane's gale,
A tail which can smash your shin
Or the legs of the chair you're in.
In spite of her awful appendage,
This dog gives the family great friendage,
And I love her a lot even though
Her tail delivered a deathblow
To my valuable antique chess set
Quite rendering it obsolesset
And an andiron and the bellows
On the hearth, and two Punchinellos
I'd bought in a small shop in Rome
And proudly displayed in my home.
And the hinge of our dishwasher
And the bowl where I serve my briocher
And the glass on our old storm door
And my grandfather's humidor
And the keyboard of my computer
(Doing that, she could not have been cuter
As that tail pounded endless F
And then broke the board right in heff.)
You'd think all this tail stuff would hurt her
But there's just no way to divert her
From wagging that great mighty club
And blasting my stuff to its nub.
Now guard well your ankle bone
'Cause her tail has a life of its own.
And I think I should oughtta warn
You that Emma's no unicorn;
'Cause to all it's really quite clear
That it's not from her head, but her rear

That the damage comes when she wags
And turns my home into rags.
So watch out when Emma's schleppin'
'Cause that tail is a lethal weapon.
And if by some chance dear Emma
Lost that tail? Oh the dilemma!
Not for me, (I'd be glad,) but for Emma.

FALLING STARS, DYING STARS

*T*he family went camping, as they always did
Each summer in August when he was a kid
They went up to Maine to the ocean and such
Where they'd roast corn and clams, and eat way too much.
At night they'd sit by the fire and sing
And they'd all laugh and talk about everything.
His name was Sam and he'd always remember
Those happy Maine trips straight through to September.
Sam and his brothers and sisters would play
On the sand, in the ocean day after day.
Sam and his siblings would gather up shells
And sea glass from the beach, and breathe in the smells
Of the blue diamond ocean which lay like a spread
And laughed as the gulls looped and brayed overhead.
His parents would rent a small boat with a sail
From which they'd fly a huge kite with a tail
They'd pack up and bring a grand picnic lunch
Of chicken and salads and sweet cakes and punch.
They'd sail to an island and there they would stay,
Exploring and eating; they'd nap and they'd play.
Then back at the campsite they'd sit by the fire
Again where they'd talk of what they'd aspire
To do with their lives in the years that remained
To them all. They knew in those summers they gained
Important life lessons; they learned about love,

The importance of family, trust and above
All else they learned how much family matters
That without a family one's life could be tatters.
But during those summers there was just one thing
That worried Sam's folks, it was never-ending;
It was on those Maine nights, so cool and so clear
(And it constantly happened year after year,)
When Sam's family at night stared up at the stars
And tried to find Mercury, Venus or Mars
The stars in the Maine sky were thick and so near
They'd all reach to grab them, but they'd reappear
In great clouds of silver and sparkle and gold
And Sam's family would gasp at the billionfold
Of heavenly bodies for them to survey
Lingeringly, longing to hold back the day.
But Sam would never look up at the sky
And his family could never figure out why.
They asked him, pleaded to tell them the reason
Why Sam wouldn't look at the stars in that season
Of beautiful summer, the nights were so fair
The moon was pure silver, hung high in the air.
"Why Sam?" his family would ask him each year
"Why won't you count the stars with us, my dear?"
"Oh, please do not make me," Sam pleaded with them.
"I have my reasons, but it's not a problem.
"Just don't make me do it, and one day I'll tell
"I promise I'll do that, then all will be well.
"It's something I thought of some time long ago
"And now I can't shake it, but you all should know
"It's nothing I can't overcome if I try
"And I try, I do, and I'd like to reply
"To your questions of why I won't look at the stars
"And try to find with you Pluto and Mars.
"But I can't do it now, tho one day I shall
"So please do not ask me. Oh please, be a pal!"
So his family stopped asking. Time passed and then

The kids were all grown. The trips came to an end.
Years and years later when the family met
For a holiday, they asked Sam his secret
He sat down and looked at them all with a smile
And said, "Sure, I'll tell you. It's been a long while
"Now it sounds silly, but it sure wasn't then
"It started way back, before I was ten
"And I used to look up at the sky every night
"And try to count stars, and I so loved the sight.
"But it seemed every time I looked up there
"In the beautiful night, that wondrous black air
"A star would shoot past, seem to fall to the ground
"The sight made me turn and run fast, homeward bound.
"A shooting star always fell straight to the earth
"And the sight of that hardly filled me with mirth.
"I began to obsess that each time I looked high
"A star would immediately fall down from the sky.
"I was so frightened, so young and unwise
"That each time, I thought, when I looked at those skies
"One more star might die and I could not bear
"For that to happen, so I had to forswear
"I'd never again stare up at the night
"And kill all the stars, and kill the starlight.

"I know I was young, but it seemed to be true
"That each time I looked up into the blue
"Of the night a great star would shoot into space
"And die! There was no way that I could replace
"That wonderful star. It was all my fault
"That it died up there, way up high in the vault.
"So I wouldn't look up when all of you did
"I'd turn on my stomach, my face down, and hid.
"I know now I was just so young and so small
"I know now that I couldn't cause stars to fall
"So now my dear family, now that I'm grown up
"You finally know why I could not look up
"At stars with you during our wonderful times
"Together when camping in those summertimes."
So finally they knew why their dear brother
Turned his head down, there could be no other
Thing he could do when they looked at the stars
Trying to locate Mercury or Mars.
He was afraid when he looked at the sky
That he'd cause the stars way up there to die
And he knew his dear family loved them all so
That he kept his head down so the stars could still glow.

BIRTHDAY GREETINGS TO FRED STEWART

Fred Stewart's a wonderful guy
He looks you straight in the eye
He's jaunty and thin
And neat as a pin
And he'll never tell you a lie.
        Fred Stewart could be a twin
of Doug Fairbanks! He could stand in
For Doug in a flick
Making ladies lovesick
And also to blush and grin.

Fred Stewart's a guy who loves cars
And if he wrote his memoirs
A lot of the words
Would be about herds
Of cars he's owned over the y'ars.
    Fred Stewart's a man who bakes bread
From recipes kept in his head
His bread is nutrish
And always delish
But mighty fatt'ning it's said.
    Fred Stewart's a wonderful man
To Doris a splendid husban'
Father and grandpop
And even great-grand-top
There ain't no chap better than!
    Fred Stewart heads a great clan
And all his kin loves this good man
Too many to count
But they're paramount
In his life, since it all began.
    Fred Stewart is now ninety three
A matter which fills him with glee!
He looks about fifty
Dapper and nifty
He simply defines bonhomie.

    I wish Happy Birthday to you
      Fred Stewart, you're always brand new!
      To me Dapper Dan
      Oh, you are the Man!
      Have a great day, Buckaroo!

SQUIRRELS

I lie in my bed in the dark of the dawn
And hear those squirrels running above.
They're up on my roof, now bored of the lawn,
(For these beasts I don't have much love.)

I lie in my bed long before it is light
And I hear those squirrels misbehave.
They dash 'cross my roof, and I ask them outright,
"Is that how you'll sound on my grave?"

MY FLOWER

I had a monkey named Flower, once
A sweet little thing was she
She performed the cutest of stunts
And gave so much pleasure to me.
     I ordered her from a pet store man
And paid him a lot of cash
The day she arrived I all but ran
To the shop and got there in a flash.
     And there she was, my new little pet
In her cage, so scared, so small.
"Spider monkey" the shopkeeper said
"Now take her," and that was all.
     He never gave me a book to read
On how to care for this beast
He had no clue as to what to do
He didn't care in the least.
     "I'll name her Flower," I told the guy
Who said "I don't wanna be blunt,
"But in that cartoon, and this is no lie,
"'Flower' was really a skunk."
     "Well I don't care," I said, now incensed

"I'll name her 'Flower,' that's that!"
I picked up the cage and then commenced
To leave, not wanting to chat.

  My boyfriend came to drive me home
And while we were going along
Flower escaped and began to roam
'Round the car, where she didn't belong.

  My boyfriend stopped and began to shriek,
Pulled his knees up to his chin.
I laughed so hard I could not speak!
He created a terrible din.

  I finally caught the cute little monk
And got her back in her cage
And then I planned how I would dump
This jerk who was in such a rage.

  I would not have a man in my life
Who wouldn't love my small beast
I'd never consent to be his wife,
Unless he liked Flower, at least.

  So life went on and I'm sad to say
I learned I'd made a mistake.
I read about the horrible way
Baby monkeys are fast overtaked.

  Men shoot a net gun over a tree
That's filled with monks and offspring.
Now trapped, the mothers struggle and scream
Clutching babes who cry and cling.

  But they can't save them try as they might
These men have much money to make.
The mothers put up a terrible fight
But those guys have too much at stake.

  You see, they can make a pot of cash
With each baby monkey they seize
The animals shriek, struggle and thrash
And most die when they're shipped overseas.

  A large amount of these precious monks

Who die will be thrown overboard.
Their kidnappers, greedy and vicious punks
Don't care. They'll make money to hoard.
   They're stuffed into crates where they can't
    breathe
They're given no water or food.
Some die when they struggle to get free
It's a horror of huge magnitude.
   Wild creatures, I've learned, I'm sad to say
Are routinely captured and then
Are sold to those who think it's OK
To cage them or keep them penned.
   These poor creatures then typically die
An awful and lonely demise
And I just cannot understand why
This brutality stays legalized.
   I've never again bought a new pet
That came from a wild, free place
And it still gets me awfully upset
That pet stores sustain this disgrace.
   I brought my sweet monk to the zoo one day
Where I knew she'd live happily
And it was such fun to see her play
With the other monks merrily.
   I went to see Flower quite often
And smiled watching her at play
The loss of my pet was quite softened
By seeing her flourish each day.
   I wish I had just never done such
A terrible thing to a beast
But I didn't know, and now much
I have learned, to say the least.
I tell you with very much joy
That Flower lived long at the zoo.
And I'm happy I didn't destroy
That dear monkey, and now, aren't you?

SORRY

I recall one very sad day when I
Crashed my car into a butterfly.
He was in his very own air space
And I was in my very own car place.
And I feel very bad that
He ended up the one splat.
Now he's just gross squishodize
And I wish I could apologize.

G BEFORE L

I knew a man who could never say the letter L
A thing which for most of us would be a living hell.
Well, he really could say the letter L, but not quite.
Whenever he had to use the letter L, despite
His toughest determination, he couldn't say it
Without putting a G in front. He could not break it.
And so he accepted his lot, telling everyone
That lots of people had it far worse. He'd carry on.
It wasn't every L he said G before. Only
Certain ones; in the midst of words, the ends, usually.
Sometimes when certain words come up with L's, they're
    just L's.
Like he'd never say a G before the L in "bells."
But soon he became quite proud of this impediment.
Figuring he was unique. He was not diffident
At all. He became vain and tried to get letter L
Into every possible sentence. He did it well!
"I glove you," he'd say to his wife. "You're my begloved."
His poor wife was becoming frazzled. She felt smuth-ed.
"I'll be glate," he'd say when he called. "There's a deglay
"In traffic. Sorry dear. Oh Glord, this has been a day!"
The couple had a lot of kids and he gave them names

All beginning with the letter L. He had no shame.
First came Glaura, then Glou-Ann, then Bglake, Glary, and
    Glink.
Cared he if they were chagrined? He didn't give a bglink!
He then bought two dogs, and named them Glassie and
    Gladdie
And laughed when he had the chance to say, "Oh yes!
    Gladgly."
He liked when he broke his toe so he could say "I glimp."
His long suffering wife thought "What a jerk. What a simp."
He begged her to move to Glouisiana, but she
Said "no, it's bad enough we have to live in Fort Glee."
"Well," he said, "One day I want to travel to Glovegland
"And Tripogli and Gagliglee, Coglorado and
"Glots of pglaces, glike the big Statue of Gliberty."
"You know dear," said his wife Gliegla. "I don't think you
    see
"You can cure this G before L thing you seem to like
"Saying so much. A speech doctor will help. Think you
    might
"Go to see one? I HATE that sound!" She'd begun to yell.
"Tut-tut! Not gladyglike," he grinned. She yelled "Go to
    hell!"
And so they parted, he and his wife. She could not take
That sound any longer. She thought her poor head would
    break.
But he would not get help, no matter how she begged, so
She took the kids and every single thing in toto,
Got a divorce and married a guy who was the norm
And spoke normally. He was kind and his love was warm.
Her Ex went on with things. He missed his kids but called
    them.
They talked til that G L sound made them mad, so they'd
    end
Those conversations with their speech-handicapped
    father

Who refused to try to rid himself of the bother.
He happily was able to make it transpire
To make numerous speeches, making folks perspire
As they tried hard to understand the strange way he'd
    speak
Wondering "Are we hearing Lithuanian? Greek?"
Here's a sample of what he'd say in his weird speeches;
"Gladies and Gentglemen, I'd glike to speak of gleeches."
Or, "Now glet's expglore, through sglides, my trip to
    Aglaska."
Or, "Glook, would you rather see my sglides of Nebraska?"
He died, glad he hadn't hidden his anomaly
From his co-workers, friends, and mainly his family.
He'd planned his tombstone, and here are the words he
    had cut;
"Here glies Glloyd Glarson, gloving famigly man, perfect but
"For a tiny defect. That's what glife is, bglemished.
    Fglawed.
"Yet that keeps it interesting. Don't get overwrought.
"I'll be cglear. Be soglid in your begliefs. Don't ever
"Give up. If you're unique, turn it into a glever
"To raise you to the stars. I promise you'gll have it made.
"Remember, if glife hands you glemons, make glemonade."

NEEDLES AND LEAVES

*D*o you think pine trees get jealous
Over leaf trees in the fall?
'Cause the leaf trees get those colors
Holding all the world enthrall.

Do you think leaf trees get jealous
Of the pine trees they behold?
'Cause pines don't have to get naked
When the world turns icy cold.

My Ghost

I don't want to boast
But I danced with a ghost
One soft and gentle eve.
     I was all alone
Nobody was home
He was not make believe.
     He streamed through the door
I could not ignore
The beauty of this wraith.
I was unafraid
And smiled when he laid
His sheer hand upon my face.
     "Dance with me," he said
I said "But you're dead!
He laughed like silvered glass.
     He swirled and he twirled
His skin was like pearl
His robes like isinglass.
     He held out his hand
And the music began
From where I have no clue.
     He floated toward me
I reached and could see
Through him, then through and through.
     The music was sweet
I felt my heart beat
In time with the harmony
     My ghost held me light
The moon, glowing bright,
Poured down like golden honey.
     "Why are you with me?"
I asked him and he
Said "I was lonesome tonight.

"I wanted to dance
"Saw you at a glance
"Standing lone in the earthlight."
        "Yes I was alone,"
"My heart felt like stone
"My lover had died, you see.
        "I'm sad and I ache
"I can't seem to shake
"This mood of melancholy."
        "Ah ha," my ghost smiled
"Then let's dance a while
"And I'll get you back some cheer."
        Then he spun me 'round
His see-through robes wound
'Bout me, and he held me near.
        My core lightened then
And I asked him when
My heart would finally heal.
        He laughed as we danced
And I felt entranced.
I heard my own laugh peal.
        We danced on and on
To the edge of dawn
And all the while my ghost crooned.
He soothed my sore soul
And made me feel whole
As we swayed under the moon.
        My heart felt so pure
I said "Are you sure
"You're really a ghost, good sir?"
        "Oh yes," said he back
"My earth name was Jack,"
And I stopped still in mid whirl.
        I looked up at him
My eyes instant brimmed
With tears of awful surprise

"You should not make jokes
"At sad grieving folks,
"Or make up terrible lies.
    "The love of my life
"Was Jack, I'm his wife
"A fact I suspect you knew."
    "I did," smiled my ghost
As he slid round a post
And his eyes were twinkled blue.
    He grinned wide at me
Then laughed with such glee
I didn't know what to think.
    "Now, why do you giggle?"
I asked, then he wiggled
And shot me a merry wink.
    "My job here tonight
"Was to give you delight,
"To help you over your pain.
    "And a message I bring
"On an angel's wing
"From Jack, your cherished swain.
    "He says 'Do not fear!
'I'm so happy here
'Though I miss you awfully much.
    'Laugh all you can
'And ignore the span
'Between us. We still can touch.
    'Call me with your heart
'And though we're apart
'I'll hear and answer true.
    'And soon, dear, I swear
'We once more will share
'All time, and our dear love too.'"
    I looked at my ghost
And said "That's the most
"Happy I've felt in a while.

"I'm glad you saw Jack
"But wish he were back
"Here. And then I'd smile."
My ghost looked me close
Said "Don't be morose,
"Laugh! It's what your Jack wants."
  "You know a great deal
"Of how Jack would feel,
"I think you're a dilettante!"
  "Look close at me, dear,"
My ghost pulled me near
And I peered into his face.
  I gasped "Now I see!"
My sad heart flew free!
And I wept in that fair place.
  This ghost was my Jack
He'd chose to come back
To tell me he was Okay.
  To quiet my grief.
It's now my belief
He wished to show me the way.
  "I just could not see
"That you were he
"When you swept me up to dance!
  "I thank you, dear love
"You came from above
"So I could have a good chance
  "To heal from your death
"To now draw each breath
"With joy. Oh thanks for this time!"
  It's hard to explain
How quickly my pain
Then vanished, like a rung chime.
  My ghost faded back,
My sweet, darling Jack
Left me alone in the night.

But now I was glad
And no longer sad
Now I smiled in the moonlight.
　　　"Thank you," I called
to my ghost, then I bawled
But they were tears of bliss.
　　　I heard him call back
"Remember your Jack!
"Now catch, I send you a kiss!"
　　　The music got soft
While Jack went aloft
I waved and then cried out,
　　　"I'll see you real soon
"Please, wait by the moon
"And never, ever doubt
　　　"That I loved you fair
"And now I can bear
"That you're gone. I love you Jack."
　　　And I heard my ghost cry
As he sailed to the sky
"I love you too. I'll be back."

MY JUNGLE

*Y*ou know what I'd do if I were rich?
And had too much money count?
I'd build myself my own little niche
And building it would be paramount
To my life! I'd have to see it done
To follow a dream I've had,
A very old dream which I had spun
As a kid, sketched on a notepad.
I'd live in a house, a normal home
On a couple of acres of land.
This place would be my halidome

This place would be my dreamland.
But back to the part about being rich.
Here's what I'd do with the money;
I'd build myself a huge glass room which
Would be dazzling and airy and sunny.
A greenhouse, really, is what it would be
But one you could sit in all day.
I'd have in there every kind of tree
And the scents would be a bouquet
From dazzling flowers blooming all year
Clustered and tiered and abounding.
I'd import them from far, maybe Kashmir
And would sit midst their beauty surrounding.
I'd have creatures live in my great glass room
Like turtles and lizards and such
And I'd have a pond with maybe some loons
And rare fish, and tree frogs in a clutch.
I'd raise butterflies in my glass dome
They'd come from all over the world.
And rare snakes and insects I'd bring to this home
And bright birds to twitter and twirl.
The floor would be marble, white, I think
My chairs white wicker for sure
With green and blue pillows, yellow and pink
And glass tables for gourmet du jour.
And servants would slide silently in
And request what I wanted to drink
I'd lazily ask that they grant my whim,
"Please bring me mint juleps," I'd wink.
The air would be heavy, sultry and damp
And I'd breathe very strongly of it.
The lush greens, rich colors, the glow-worm's lamp
All wondrous, and oh how I'd love it.
I'd have a net hammock where I'd take a nap
In the dappled green light of the day
Maybe I'd doze, maybe not or mayhap

I'd watch all my creatures at play.
The best thing about this glass home of mine
Would be when the winter would bite.
I'd sit smugly in my tropical shrine
And love seeing green before white.
So this is my dream, my own sweet pie slice
To get it, there's only one hitch.
For me to get this sublime paradise
I'd first have to get really rich.

OH NO, YOU TELL HIM

*W*hy does it have to be so difficult?
And why is it just too horrificult?
Why do we have such trouble saying it?
How come we just keep on delaying it?
Why do we fidget and keep on hopin'
Someone else will tell him his fly's open?

FINAL WISHES

*L*ast week I dressed in my Sunday best
To go see an old friend laid to rest.
Not much to look at in her lifetime
And she never became a wife, I'm
Sad to say they gussied her up
To look like a clown. They whirled up
Her hair in towering, frothy puff
And covered her face with tons of stuff
Like rouge, mascara and shimm'ring gloss
Which on her quite simply looked like dross
Applied with a large spackle knife
She looked as if she'd led the wild life.
She looked kaleidoscopely waxy

(And while she lived she wasn't saxy.)
They'd tried to make her like a starlet
But made her like an aging harlot.
I stared unbelieving at my old friend
And thought "how could they vilipend
"This simple woman, plain and good?
"And make her look like painted wood?"
I went home filled with resolution
To tell our sons of my solution
On what to do when I cork off;
"Cook a pot of stroganov
"And have a party in my name
"And laugh and say 'she was some dame!'
"Don't bury me on precious land
"The earth's already far too jammed.
"Recycle what's still good to use
"And burn the rest, and don't abuse
"My wish to not be on display
"My face all smeared with gaudy clay
"My hair done up in ways I never
"Did it. I was just not clever
"In the ways of fashion, coiffure
"I never was la mode du jour.
"I love you kids, so please, won'tcha
"Obey my wishes, or I'll hauntcha."

FIREFLIES

2 4 6 11 12 15
I was counting fireflies early one iffning.

12 13 14 7 — or was that 10?
Hey! Am I counting some over again?

71

MONEY

$\mathcal{D}$on't you often just want to earnestly punch out those
    fools who say
"Money is not important at all in absolutely no way"?
When even to anyone with the brain of a flattened souffle
Money is the most important thing there is on any one
    day.
They don't like food? Shelter? Warm clothes? A nice car?
    No? Then I'd say
For them it's true. Money is NOT important. Let them
    sleep in hay
And starve, be naked and cold and walk about on bare
    feet so they
Can show the world they're so brave, that money makes
    a person decay.
Let them gaze at the stars and trees and sun and moon
    and let them bray
About how those are the best things in life because
    they're free, OK?
Let them go a few days without food and warmth because
    they can't pay
Let them sleep in the snow and then feast on some nice
    free worms or clay
And never earn an honest dime, and mock people who
    earn their way
So they can have all those wonderful things in life so they
    can stay
Healthy, happy, free of disease, and after a day's work can
    play
With their healthy, happy, educated children who are that
    way
Because their families have money to keep them fit from
    their birthday
And on through the rest of their lives til they've grown
    and moved away.

It seems to me it's quite often
   wealthy people who love
   to say
That money has no impor-
   tance. They seem to not
   care that they betray
All the people in the world
   who are poor and who work
   hard all day.
So when those morons say
   "Money? Important? Oh no, in no
   way!"
        Damn fools, I say.

SOAP MYSTERIES

*W*henever I stay at a nice motel
Or at an inn or a fancy hotel
I cannot enjoy myself and here's why;
The reason is pretty cut-and-dry.
You know those cakes of soap they have there?
So small you hardly can get a lathere?
Since we just use half and never save 'em
And leave them behind on the basin
What happens to all those used bars of soap?
Who takes them? Someone who needs them, I'd hope.
And where do they store those wet hairy cakes?
Do they take them back home for soap grubstakes?
Do they send them to a huge vat someplace
To be melted down so they can replace
Them in the hotel rooms that I stay in
So I can be worried about this a-gin?

The Horse on the Ribbon

That Fall was the sort we hadn't much seen
In so many years, more than seventeen!
It lasted much longer than most Falls do
Delighting our senses before it was through.
The colors exploded all over the land
Detonated rainbow and firebrand.
The sky was the color of Aunt Min's sapphire
The sun a gold disk of spinning wildfire.
We took a long drive to see it all
Before winter started its vicious crawl.
We drove past a farm high on a knoll
And what I saw thrilled my weary soul.
A great horse ran 'round in circles wide
The sun and the sky gleamed from his black hide.
He glistened, he shimmered and tossed his head high
He snorted and pranced and rolled his dark eye.
His mane and his tail rippled and flowed
When he cantered, trotted, galloped or strode.
What kept this great black from charging away
From that knoll on that farm on that beauteous day
Was his spotless white halter, from it flowed a band
Of shining blue satin, its end in the hand
Of a lovely tall girl dressed in white pants
And a gossamer shirt which at a glance
Appeared to be the very same hue
As the ribbon which held the horse. It was blue.
And so were her eyes, quite easily seen
For their brightness; less blue, more aquamarine.
The young girl's long hair gleamed bright in the sun
Black, like her horse's, and she watched him run
Round and round at the end of his lead
Tossing and snorting, this strong, mighty steed.
We slowed down and stopped and stared at this sight
Of this dance these two did in that dazzling light.

They seemed to hear music, their own, rarefied
She moved her lithe body in time with his stride.
The brilliant fall leaves and the brilliant fall skies
Shone on the horse, and her hair; from her eyes.
And her ebony hair! Against those fall trees
The contrast was lovely! It swung in the breeze.
The young girl laughed and called to her beast
And he reared and he whinnied, quite clearly pleased
With himself, his power and great beauty, too
And the girl laughed aloud at their odd pas de deux.
The sun spilled down gold on the horse's blue lead
It turned to blue silver while guiding the steed.
The girl's bright blue shirt and wondrous blue eyes
Matched that long ribbon, matched those clear skies.
We smiled at the girl as she exercised
Her great muscled horse with his gleaming black hide.
The blue of that ribbon, her shirt and her eyes
Radiant contrast with leaves, and those skies.
We hated to leave that stunning display
Of beauty and nature and color that day.
The vision of blues and shimmering black
And vivid, bright leaves exploding in back.
But we had to stop watching. We had to get home.
How we hated to leave what we'd been shown.
That girl and her horse at their private play
Made something special on that special day.
And I'm sad that I'll never again see the sight
Of a girl and her horse in that wondrous Fall light.

OUT, DAMNED SPLINTER

Life gives us many aggravations, but one I find inordi-
    nately unsoothing,
And it's this; splinters frequently enter us in places
    impossible for removing.

In A Word

*I*t is a fabulous book
Written by Mr. Jack Hitt
It's name? "In A Word,"
And everyone's heard
To discover new words, this book's it!

Now these words are never found
In normal dictionaries.
They are mostly weird
But none are dog-eared
'Cause they're new, they're accretionaries!

I'll give you some examples
Of Hitt's outrageous words
Some he's invented
Some he's augmented
And a few he's expanded by thirds.

One of them is "horicious"
A really wonderful term
It means "It's just great"
Also "second rate,"
And there are others I can confirm.

How about a "goobermensch?"
Now this word's a kind of strain.
It means one who needs
To be one who leads
But to everyone he's a mere bane.

I found another great word
It's "story-eyed," am I right?
It means looking pure

While lying for sure
Making people think black is white.

And here's another for you
I like this one a whole lot.
It is "fruth," or "frue"
It means false and true
Like some things on the tube; tommyrot!

A specially ghastly word
"Berumptotfreude." Please abide.
It means finding cheer
And to even jeer
When a real famous person has died.

Indeed this is a fine book
Those words! I love to reveal 'em!
I love each new word
Tho lots are absurd
I'm a writer, so I'll likely steal 'em!

O WAY DOWN SOUTH IN LOOZYANNA

I don't think I'd wanna
Live in Loozyanna
'Cause it's too darned hot down there.
I don't think I'd wanna
Live in Loozyanna
'Cause I don't know squat 'bout there.
But maybe I'd wanna
Live in Loozyanna
'Cause they've got pralines down there.
And maybe I'd wanna
Live in Loozyanna
'Cause they've got N'Orleans down there.

IF

*I*f the stars could sing, how would they sound?
Like crystal platinum, I'll be bound.
If trees could dance, how could they do that?
(After dancing, they'd put their roots back.)
If clouds could paint, which colors to choose?
That's pretty clear; golds and blues.
If dogs could ski, how would they do that?
Maybe with a yellow or a blue cat.
If, to a cow, drinking tea was a dream,
Would they like it with lemon or cream?
If bees could talk and called you friend,
Would they warn you of their back end?
If turtles climbed trees and got stuck up there,
Would you look around for a cop somewhere?
If a skunk makes love to his heart's delight
And his tail shoots up, should she take flight?
If cactus could turn into a rocking chair
Would you want to sit and rock there?
If a matinee idol held you in his arms
I'll bet you wouldn't sound the alarms.
If words in a book could jump to your plate
Would you swallow them down and not hesitate?
If poison ivy turned into roses
Would people smell it with their noses?
If water could turn into tonic and gin
Would you be the first to shower in?
If I now promised to end this poem
Would you sigh with relief and run for home?

WOMEN IN PANTS, MEN IN SKIRTS

I stood on the sidewalk
Amongst many folks
While we waited to see the start
Of the year's big parade
I'd looked forward to
It began at the shopping mart.
Some men were behind me
And I heard them laugh
When a heavy woman walked by.
The worst of those dunces,
The coarsest of all
Made gross reference to her backside.
I turned in a fury
And I glared at him
But that type could not care less.
He laughed in my face
And said something more,
Like "women in pants are a mess.
"They look like fat hippos
"They waddle like ducks,"
And his minions then laughed with glee
They were not Adoni
They were simply slobs
These morons in soiled dungaree.
Their bellies were massive
Their shirts thickly stained
And they wore filthy baseball caps.
Their hair was quite long
And greasy and snarled
I'll bet all they did was shoot craps.
And finally the parade
Began with a bang
And it was a kick to behold.

The costumes were shiny
The music a joy
I was thrilled at the rigmarole.
And then came the bagpipes
My favorite part
The sound of them just makes me cry.
Those Scottish musicians
Made their mighty pipes
Blast music straight up to the sky.
I watched with some interest
As those pipers passed
A few of them really were fat.
Those critical cretins
All standing near me
Sneered loud at those guys. Think of that!
But not, I observed
Because they were stout
But because they wore the kilt.
"Hey look! Skirts on guys!"
They belched loud through their beers
And those fools they drooled, all atilt.
But I never heard them
Utter one statement
About the good pipers' backsides
Which vied the large women's
Who wore those tight pants
Those men in kilts looked like shipsides.
The standard is double
I am sad to say
Those slobs did not feel any guilts
They believed it okay
To mock a fat miss
In pants, not a fat guy in kilts.

My Lake

Living on a lake is the thing, you see.
A house by a lake is the place for me.
I won't get that chance, and never will
I'm just too old now, I'm over the hill.
But when I drive by a sun sparkled lake
It tugs at my soul, a sense I can't shake.
My throat thickens hard, my eyes fill with tears
And slowly I back-slide through all the years.
Alone on a lake the color of sky
There was only one sound, my happy sigh.
I'm in a grey boat, all creaky and old
The oars are worn warm, like shell in my hold
I pull on them hard. They bend and complain
I slide o'er the top of my water domain.
The ends of the oars make magical whirls
In the dark satin water, spinaway swirls.
The sound of the water lapping the sides
Of my boat is music, played summertide.
The soft air-wind's spun with cobwebs and glass
I drowse in the sun while dragonflies pass
Cicadas on shore with Mourning Doves call
They sing to me, beckon, hold me in thrall.
My fingers drift down and over the side
And slide through the water where fishes hide.
With slender legs the waterbugs scribble
Surface designs, and I feel faint nibble
Of tender fish mouths, it's how they greet me.
They think "there's no hook. She'll never eat me."
And I wouldn't, I couldn't dine on my friends
Polliwogs, turtles, and fish are Godsends.
I pull in my oars and let the boat drift
To the side of the lake where I then lift
My lazy eyes to the best of all scenes,
The edge of the lake. In all shades of greens

And browns, and blues, and mysterious hue.
There's much to discover, a wondrous stew
Of turtles, minnows, and frogs and the like
Enchanted kingdom of water and light.
I reach down quite low and feel with my hand
The lake bottom's silky dark fairyland.
I hang o'er the side, I can't get my fill
Of that world down there of lake creature spill.
My boat drifts some more and I do not care
If I vanish from sight in the sun's glare.
My boat bumps gently against the soft bank
And the smell of the air is mellow/sweet dank.
I hide there amongst the roots and the rocks
There are no people, other boats or docks.
The gentle waves try to rock me to sleep
And I nearly succumb to their calm sweep.
Green branches bend low and keep me well hid
From the world. And as I drift there amid
The shadowed, sun dappled creature-filled lake
I float in daydream. I pray not to wake.
I love being here, alone on this lake
And think when I'm old and scared, I'll betake
Myself in my mind to this blissful place
And life will return to calmness and grace.
Yes a lakeside house is the thing for me
A home by a lake is the place to be.
But now it's too late, I'm over the hill
I did get there once, but now never will.

MY WAY OF EXERCISING

I know by today's standards of health that this will sound
like I'm an insalubrious herotic;
But I think the walking-from-computer-to-bed workout as
being a high impact aerobic.

FROM LEBANON WITH LOVE

I've happily eaten Chinese
And dined on common Burmese
And loved every smidgen of it.
I 'specially love Italian
And sometimes I dine Bacchanalian.
And oft rediscover I love it.
I've et food from the land of Thai
And nibbled fried snake on the sly
It tasted like chicken a bit.
I didn't feel at all woozy
The night I gobbled down sushi
And Indian cuisine was a hit!
But adoring all of these
One night I tried Lebanese
And it was a whole new thing.
The menu read like Swahili
It didn't translate too freely.
It was all really baffling.
I didn't know even one food
Offered, but I didn't brood
About my lack of knowledge.
So I asked the patient waiter
To please be the commentator
To make my meal sortilege.
He smiled and said "You must try
All our foods. They're to die!"
I agreed to try them all.
And here is the Lebanese fare
That I ate that night, and I swear
That I loved that food, overall.
I ate grape leaves and tabouli
Although I felt like a foolie
'Cause I didn't know what to call it.

I sort of knew Shish Kabob
And did a pretty good job
Of eating it (while I eye-balled it.)
But what in the heck was corfu?
Do you open it with a corkscrew?
I didn't know what to think.
And how about kibbee nayee?
(I wasn't making much headwayee.)
Was it something to eat or to drink?
Babaghanouj I could not pronounce
(But hummus I'll always denounce,)
My head had started to spin.
Should I try some of the falafel?
(It smelled sort of good to my nostril.)
I hoped it was not toxin.
I thought I'd try something kabob
A kafta thingamabob
It really tasted so good!
The waiter suggested tawook
So I said I'd take a look
And would eat it in all likelihood.
And then he suggested shankleesh
To which I responded "oh sheesh!"
I was at this point awfully full.
He said, "But you must try rice curry!"
And with a very fine flurry
He plopped down a platterful.
That Lebanese food was a feast
An agape, to say the least!
I wouldn't have missed a crumb!
"Lebanese coffee?" the waiter suggested
With arak I then ingested
Which rendered my tongue quite numb!
I'd have to look at a map
To see where Lebanon's at
I'm shamed to have to confess.

But wherever it is, their cuisine
Is definitely fit for a queen
(OK, I sometimes obsess.)
If you can't even do the IDs
Of the foods in the Leb's recipes
Do something for you that will please;
When one night you want to dine out
And you can't think which food to try out
Don't falter. Go eat Lebanese.

LENORA LEE

*H*er name was Lenora Lee
And Lenora was lovely.
And he loved Lenora Lee
But Lenora didn't love he.
    Her long hair was raven black
Her eyes like mellow cognac
Her voice? Ah, sheer Dvorak
She always smelled of lilac.
    Oh how his heart would ache
Each time Lenora Lee spake.
He knew his heart would break
If that heart she wouldn't take.
    He asked her out for a meal
And hoped she'd accept with zeal.
But she laughed and said "No deal!"
She made him feel like a heel.
    Sweet Lenora Lee and he
Worked side by side making Brie.
One day while he stirred the cheese
He threw himself down on his knees.
    "Oh please dear Lenora Lee
"Please say that you'll marry me!"
The girl stopped stirring the Brie

And said "Oh, I can't marry."
    He stood then, and said "Why not?
"I haven't got a lot
"But I have more than one pot
"And money, things and what-not."
    "Oh dear," said Lenora Lee
"You just cannot marry me!
"I work hard making this Brie
"To feed the parents of me."
    "Support your parents you do?
"You pay their rent, feed them too?
"Lenora, I never knew!
"I'm glad I found out! Oh, phew!
    "And if you and I were wed
"And set up a new homestead
"You'd bring in the aforesaid
"Parents, Adelaide and Fred?"
    "Yes," said Lenora Lee
"They'd have to come with me.
"I've made a commitment, see?"
"Yes I understand," said he.
    He wanted to marry her
But really, he'd much prefer
To live with just only her
But not with her, him and her.
    He quit his job making Brie
And went to work packing tea.
He thought of Lenora Lee
And grieved that he'd had to flee.
    He thought "She was cute-iful"
And he wept a snootiful.
Lenora Lee was beautiful
But she was much too dutiful.

THOSE ONE SHOES

*N*ot many people know this
I didn't know mysel'.
But I'd be non compos mentis
If I did not tell.
Here's the scoop dear folks
Now hold onto your peg
Our world is full of blokes
Who only have one leg.
A really well kept secret
These people want it thus
Although they cannot curvet
They'll keep it their modus
To do the things all others
Do, and do with ease
And never cause rude pothers
For them it's just a breeze.
You really cannot tell
How many are extants
They keep their secret well
'Cause they always wear long pants.
Know how I found out
So many have one limb?
Easy! I just went out
And on a simple whim
I looked around and saw
A certain travel thing
I let out a guffaw
'Twas obvious as string.
These people don't need two shoes
As they tour life's byways
So without any boo-hoos
They toss extras out on highways.

NAILS

No matter how hard I struggle
I can't ever seem to juggle
All the new fashion trends.
I'm always one step behind
The rest of human kind
No matter how good my intends.
Take fingernails for example
Like you, I've also got ample.
I decided to paint them red.
I wanted to be au courant
To grow them so I could flaunt
The fact that I too could be hep.
Of course I was far too late
As usual not up to date
I have no sartorial knack.
As soon as I painted them red
I felt like a chowder head
'Cause the girls were now painting them black.
And all that time making them grow
Was wasted, so now I know.
Oh well, life just ticks on.
Once more I'm three steps behind
'Cause now I suddenly find
Today's nails all simply stick-on.

LITTLE GIRLS

My husband and I could not ask for more
Than to have little girls living next door.
We can't wait for summer so he and I
Can open our drapes and throw windows high.
Those sweet little girls are sisters I think

But they're not always sweet, they'll yell "you stink!
"And you're just a dork, and I hate you, you pig!
"And well, you're a jerk! And a thingamajig."
The rest of the time, though, their noises are sweet
They shriek in their pool in the thick summer heat.
The laugh to hysterics when jumping up high
On their trampoline as they grab for some sky.
They giggle and joke and put on weird plays
Dress up, read books, and play games like croquet.
But the very best thing those little girls do
Is sing! You should hear them! Quite out of the blue!
I just didn't know kids still sang, don't you see?
And all a cappella! And with such esprit!
It's simply amazing to hear those dear girls
Their voices like silver that's shot through with pearls.
We wish in a way the leaves on the trees
Would come in the winter, although they would freeze.
But see, those leaves that grow thick and green
Cut our view of those girls. They're mostly unseen.
But still, we can hear their high voices in song
And sometimes my husband and I sing along!
They sing "London Bridges" and "Little Bo Peep"
and "Ring Round the Rosie," oh I could just weep!
I'd thought all those old songs were gone from this world
And hearing them sung again makes my head whirl
With memories of back when I was a child
And sang those quaint songs, so gentle, so mild.
We stand and we listen and can't get enough
Of hearing them sing, and play and do stuff.
My husband and I love the summers the best
Because we can hear those girls sing. We are blessed.
I guess no one ever can feel really poor
As long as they hear little girls sing next door.

Men on Vacation

*H*ere's a simple observance of mine
Don't call me sexist. It's just my opine.
And I know it's really not always true,
And I also know that you might argue.
But here's the deal, it's no affectation
You always can tell men who're on vacation.
I'll tell you why if you're curious
Although it'll make a lot of gents furious.
But they seem to dress in horrid apparel
When they'd really do better dressed in a barrel.
These normally well dressed men decide
To find a sweet cottage by the seaside.
Then on day one of their vacation
(They ought to be forced to deportation,)
They put on some shorts of vomitus plaid
And their shirts? The best description is "bad."
These guys who dress well on business days
Whose wildest colors are black, grey, and beige
Just lose it and suddenly they're wearing a symphony
Of baroque colors more like a timpani.
These guys seem to not feel the tiniest shame
Of walking about in shirts aflame
With Hawaiian patterns, or prints or stripes
Of mismatched splendor of ghastly types
Of every material known to man,
The clothes on these guys look like Grandma's divan.
And what's with their socks? Don't they have a clue?
Black socks and black shoes with shorts just won't do.
Especially short black socks, especially nylon
The clothes on these guys no housefly would fly on.
Some wear tank tops when they really not oughtta
Over huge bellies. They don't really gotta.
And those hats, there really should be a law

They inevitably make all viewers guffaw.
But there's one sure way you can always tell
When a man's on vacation (though he does rebel).
It's while he's shopping with his dear wife
And she's trying on clothes as if her life
Is about to end, so she'd better buy lots,
And her husband awaits her, thinking bad thoughts.
The way you can tell those poor guys on holiday?
It's clear to all, for them it's no jolly day.
They're the guys with the big sourpusses
Looking a lot like furious gooses.
They're the guys who're muttering curses.
They're the guys forced to hold their wife's purses.

SISTER BERNADETTE GETS DOWN!

*W*hen she was young she would love to sing
She'd raise her eyes while her voice took wing.
Hands on their ears, her parents would wail,
"You can't carry a tune in a pail!"
Undaunted, she smiled and said "I must!
"If I cannot sing, surely I'll bust!
"I must sing every chance I get!"
This mulish child was named "Bernadette."
"No singing on Sundays," her folks said,
"For it's a grave sin! You'll be struck dead!"
"That's silly," said the child with a grin.
"God loves singing! It can't be a sin!"
"Your singing's a sin then," said her dad,
"Completely off-key! It's really bad!"
"Sorry dear father," said she sadly,
"But God won't care if I sing badly.
"For Him it's no crime if I'm off key,
"To Him music's good, don't you see?
"It does not always have to praise Him

"All kinds of music can amaze Him."
"Well," her folks said, "Never on Sunday,
"We know for a fact that that's one day
"He'll smite you for sure, 'specially when
"You caterwaul and squawk like a hen.
"Sorry child, if we've hurt your feelings
"But your horrid songs put holes in our ceilings.
"Please sing far away, maybe go to the coast!
"But not on Sunday, or you'll be toast."
But Bernadette so loved music and God
She became a nun, and each day she'd plod
Off to her tasks, and sang as she went.
She sang all year from Easter through Lent.
The Sisters wept and prayed that she'd stop
The sound hurt their heads, made their ears pop.
But nothing could stop Sister Bernadette
She knew God approved her, and would let
Her sing loud, off-key, and yes, pantheistic
Even though the nuns were going ballistic.
Bernadette sang Rock, Hymns and Blues
And never once heard all the nuns' "Boos!"
One day the nuns bowed their cowled heads low
Toward each other and said "She must go!
"She wrecks each day with that awful sound
"Like roosters at dawn! A howling hound!
"Let's send her to a far distant shore
"And get back our silent days of yore!"
"Now Sisters," said the Reverend Mother
"We can't dump her off on some other
"Innocent folks who don't know her vice
"Sisters! You know that would not be nice!
"Let's make a deal with our screeching nun,
"Quiet her down, but let her have fun.
"Let's sound-proof her room, give her a cat
"Ask her to sing there, loudly and flat
"As she wants to, and often and much!

"And oh, dear Sisters, won't it be such
"A pleasure to have quiet anew?
"And Sister Bernadette will not rue
"That we gave her a dear little cat
"To care for and love. Now that is that!
"We'll line the walls of her room with foam
"From which Sister B. won't want to roam.
"We'll give a big couch on which she'll sit
"And sing shrilly! Perhaps even knit!
"We'll give her a radio, and oh then
"She can sing with it when she has a yen!
"We'll make it so sound-proof, comfy, snug
"She can croon loud! We won't have to plug
"Our ears any more from her vile din.
"But oh, I wish she thought it a sin
"To sing on Sundays. We know it's not,
"But we'd have sweet peace, ah! Camelot!"
All went quite well. The nuns were at peace!
They smiled a lot and now could surcease
Holding their ears from Bernadette's stir
But they still loved the nun, cared for her.
It all went badly, it's sad to say.
The Sisters were quite unnerved one day
When Sister B. came out of her room
And began singing, her voice a-boom!
"Why did you leave your room and your cat?"
Asked Reverend Mother, who thought "Oh drat!"
"I do appreciate all you did,"
Said Sister B., "And oh, God forbid
"I know you'll think I am manic
"But alone in a room, I simply just panic.
"I've tried hard to be oh so stoic
"Sorry, but I'm quite claustrophobic."
"Oh no, Oh no!" the good Sisters cried,
Six of them wept and three of them sighed.
"Dear Sisters," Sister B. smiled and said,

"I'd no idea!" and she shook her head.
"I can see how you've missed me, and Oh!
"I am so touched, I just did not knowow.
"So my dear Sisters, to show you how
"Touched I am, I'm prepared to, right now
"Spend every mealtime and every eve,
"While you bake bread, sew, scrub and weave
"Sing to you, any song you desire!
"Solos! Duets! I'll bring in a choir!"
The Sisters groaned and wrinkled their brows
A couple said "We'll have to give up our vows!
"We swore we'd follow our dear Lord's word
"But He'd never ask this if He heard
"Sister B. sing! It's wrecking our lives!
"It's almost like perpetual shrives!"
Sister B. heard them and said "Don't fret!
"I don't have to sing! Did you forget?"
She ran to her room wearing a grin.
The Sisters heard her searching within.
Soon Sister Bernadette came back out
Smiled at the nuns and said with a shout,
"I'll sing no more! I'll be much kinder!"
They paled! There was a tuba behind her.

HATS AND MOI

I'm nuts about hats, all
  kinds, they're cool,
  but I can't wear a
  one of 'em.

My neck's too short, I
  look like a dork, so I
  can't have the fun of
  'em.

MY PRAYER

I think prayer is for the pray-er
And not really answered by God
God I think, wants us to care
For others and ourselves, does God.
We are all on our own down here
And prayer really helps us with that
And while God for sure lends His ear
I don't think He wants to chit-chat.
It's all up to us, you see
To make a good life while here
For God makes no guarantee
That life will be sweet or severe.
But knowing all that I still pray
A small simple prayer every night
And here's what I always say;
(Who knows if God listens? He might!)
"Hi God," I say just before sleep
"If you are responsible for
"This fine, past day that I'll keep
"In my heart forevermore
"Then I thank you for that, dear God.
"May I ask You for one more gift?
"Can you answer before I nod?
"You say 'yes,' and my heart will lift!
"You refuse, and I'll feel great sorrow,
"Til now You've said 'yes,' it is so;
"May I have one more day tomorrow?"
(I know that one night You'll say no.)

ORANGE ORANGES

*M*y hero, the dear, lovely Ogden Nash
Quite often wrote joyful balderdash.
He wrote tons and tons of wondrous verses
Without any violence, sex or curses.
But there was one word he could not rhyme
They tell me he spent his whole lifetime
Trying to chase this elusive word.
It's one we all know, it's commonly heard.
It's "orange." It's said it can't be rhymed,
Can't even be easily pantomimed.
I'm going to try to give it a shot
Although it may sound like tommyrot.
(Now Ogden up there, don't curl up your toes
Here's my poor effort. OK now. Here goes:)
"The sunset that eve was growing oranger
"While he ate porridge from his porringer."

THE SISTER AND HER RAINBOW

*O*nce upon a time there was a little nun
Who lived life for God, but had little fun.
"God doesn't want me to be melancholy,"
She thought, "He'd rather I really be jolly!"
So she took orphaned kids to see happy plays
And also to ball games, to beaches to laze.
The little nun loved that, but something was wrong
Something was missing. In her heart was no song.
"Ah me," sighed the nun, "I guess I'm just greedy,
"The Lord's just so good, I'm just much too needy."
The little nun made up her mind to forget
About how she felt. She would no longer fret.
She made up her mind to ignore her feelings
And pray to the Lord to grant her some healings.

She'd work hard by day and would pray hard by night
And would work hard too, and do what was right.
One summer day after all chores were done
She sat on a bench and drowsed in the sun.
Startled, she jumped when she heard a strange sound
And looked at the sky, at the trees and all 'round.
Dazzling colors streaked past her eyes
Like apples, apricots, green grass and sunrise.
It squawked quite loudly which startled her greatly
Flew in mad circles and then pretty straightly.
And then to her shock the bird flew straight at her
And perched on her shoulder, starting to chatter.
"A parrot! A parrot!" the nun cried aloud
She reached up to stroke him, and felt very proud
This lost bird had picked her above all the others
Over the priests and the sisters and brothers.
The little nun strolled to her cell with the bird
She was laughing, weeping and everyone heard
Her say she'd work hard to find the bird's owner
And they also heard "But I'm such a loner.
"And God has sent this new friend to please me
"He'd never do this to sadden or tease me!
"He wants me to have a new friend all my own
"So I won't feel cheerless, as only He's known."
Delighted, she took the bird into her cell
And wrote out an ad for the paper to tell
The people who lost their dear parrot to call.
Then the little nun prayed and tried not to bawl.
She asked God to let no one answer the ad
And after a month she became very glad
When no one laid claim to the colorful bird
Said the nun "Oh thank you. My prayers have been heard."
Now everyone noticed how happy she was
"She's happy! She's joyous!" The nuns were a-buzz.
And no one begrudged the little nun's gladness
That gorgeous parrot removed all her sadness.

She named him "Rainbow," and everyone told her
That parrots are able to get much older.
"He'll outlive us all!" the Sisters all teased her
The little nun loved all the fuss. It pleased her!
She loved her dear Rainbow and felt very glad
That he'd live long. He was all she had.
She taught him to speak, to fetch and do tricks
And he'd steal her glasses, and crucifix.
The little nun now did her chores with a smile
And rushed through her prayers to get home to her "child."
The nun and her parrot passed such happy years
He scolded and broke things and pulled on her ears.
She clipped back his wings so he would not depart
Her darling parrot was part of her heart.
The Sisters had never seen her so happy
And laughed when she sometimes called Rainbow
    "Chappie."
"You'd best make provisions for him in your will,"
Said the Sisters, "Since parrots rarely get ill."
One morning the little nun called him to come
When he didn't answer, her heart became numb.
"Oh Rainbow, where are you?" the little nun cried
And she found him, all crumpled where he had died.
The little nun fell to the floor and she wept
And she howled and wailed and finally slept.
She dreamed that together they flew very high
Up through the clouds, and to God in the sky.
The little nun wrapped her arms 'round the bird's neck
And up they went higher, til they were a speck.
Her dear parrot carried her straight to her Lord
His bright wings flew to their well-earned reward.
The Sisters came in and approached them with dread
And burst into tears. Their dear nun friend was dead.
Her arms were wrapped tightly around her dear pet
The drops from her tears on his wings were still wet.
They buried the nun with her cherished bird

And when they had finished, her voice could be heard;
"Good-bye my dear Sisters, I'm now heaven-bound
"And dear Rainbow's with me. We'll see you around!
"I'm happy dear Sisters, God's given me much
"And now I'll be able to live hear His touch!
"I'll soar in the rapture with my sweet Chappie
"And watch over you and hope that you're happy.
"I was so sad til the parrot was sent me
"Has God ever treated a nun so gently?"
The nuns glanced around but they could not see her
But all of them to a woman could hear her.
They never doubted they heard her speak
But they knew without her, their lives would be bleak.
They held hands tightly and stood there and listened
And on each of their cheeks, many tears glistened.
The little nun's voice came floating back to them
And they listened closely, her voice did soothe them.
"I'll watch o'er you, dear Sisters and hope that soon
"You'll shortly be with me, near the sun and moon.
"And I pray if you're lonely our Lord will try
"To send you a pet so you will not cry.
"And now please excuse me, I've got to depart
"So good-bye for now and there's love in my heart
"For all of you Sisters who loved me so dear.
"Good-bye now, farewell now, my Rainbow is near
"We've got work to do, but I just want to say
"That mostly we'll fly around heaven all day!"

BOB AND I AND THE PLAZA

*A*s a husband
Bob beats all.
Good to me
And on the ball.
Feeds me, loves me

Pays my bills
Understands and
Cures my ills.
Faithful to me
Like a dog
Cooks the meals
Goes light on grog.
But Bob screwed up
One time with me.
I know he's male
But come on! Gee!
Just because
He's a guy
That's no excuse
For a blind eye.
Here's what happened
Here's the deal.
We'd been asked
Out for a meal
At the Plaza
(Tres chi chi)
With some folks
Tres tres wealthy.
My hair that day
Looked quite like hell
Swirling about
Sheer pell-mell.
And so I did
What all girls do
I stuck it down
With hairspray glue.
But still some spikes
Kept popping high
So them I clamped
With angry sigh.
I took some clips

Real ugly things
Rusted metal;
Just horridings.
I clamped the spikes
Down to my skull
Flattened the mess
And made it null.
They did the trick
And off we went
Dressed so well!
Magnificent!
We met our friends
(Real rich folk,
Her diamond rings
Were sure no joke.)
They looked at me
I looked at them
They looked stricken
Bob said "ah hem."
"What?" said I
Bob looked stunned.
"What??" I cried
I felt numb.
He nodded hard
Toward my head.
"What's your problem??"
I loudly said.
Bob kept nodding
Toward my head
"What is wrong?"
I louder said.
I reached up
And touched a clip
Still in my hair.
Then took a fit!
"Why didn't you,"

At Bob I hissed
Pointing headward,
"Remind me? This!"
Bob blanched white
And sheepish grinned
Then scoffed and said,
"OK, I've sinned."
I yanked the clips
From my hairdo
Glared and said "You'd
best never do!"
Well, looking back
I've got to say
Bob's been quite fine
From day to day.
But I cannot
Forgive him none
For seeing the clips
And staying mum.
I know he did
Not mean to goof
But I felt like
a major doof.
I can't forgive
My darling spouse
And I still think
He is a louse
For forgetting
To tell me
To pull those clips.
(I'd've told he.)
I'll never give Bob a
Tabula Rasa
Because he forgot to remind me to remove my hair clips
when we were walking through
The Plaza.

In Praise Of

The poor man couldn't speak well
His throat was hurting so
"Laryngitis hurts like hell"
He said, and I said "Oh,"
"But I wrote a verse today
I think it of my best.
"And even though it's hard to speak,
"I'd like you to attest
"To the fact that it is good
"The best I've ever written.
"A poem that I prob'ly should
"Think about submittin'.
Long suff'ring spouse could only squeak
"Well damn, I don't detest it."
I found it sudd'nly hard to speak,
"That means you just respect it?"
I said "Do you dislike my poem?"
"Well," he said, "please shove it
"In the shredder," then he groaned,
"Oh damn, I have to love it?"
"Oh, thanks a lot" I said, some curts,
"I'm sorry it's a bore."
"It's not a bore, but my throat hurts,
"Damn Damn! I don't abhor
"The poem you wrote, now let me go."
"So go!" I said with pout.
"It's hard for me to speak, you know,"
"Oh yeah, that's some cop-out,"
Said I behaving like a child.
And quickly was contriteful.
And said "I know I just get wild
"And sometimes act quite spiteful."
"Well, that's OK," dear husband hissed

"I know your verses matter."
We came together and we kissed
"OK, now no more chatter."
We'd said all that we could've stated.
I heard the car door slam.
I sighed and said "Oh, how I hate it
"When he praises with faint damn."

THE LADY'S CLOTHES MAN

*I*t had to have been a woman hater
The guy who invented that.
A real angry chap, a true mandater
Of high style, from shoes to hat.

        I think he invented girdles and then
Was thrilled when he saw they hurt,
And insisted each maiden and doyenne
Look indecent in a much too short skirt.

        But females must take much of the blame
For letting this guy dictate
That they should wear clothes which make them feel
shame
And cause pain they can't tolerate.

        This woman hater is really quite good
At creating painful clothes
But the lowest blow he dealt womanhood
Was inventing pantyhose.

MEN AND PLAIDS

*S*omething happens to men past a certain age
Something they suddenly favor. It's really awful bad.
Here's what it is; they suddenly reach the stage
Where they love wearing pants of atrocious, lurid plaid

THE PEANUTBUTTER TREE

There's a special tree in my back yard
Behind my house on the boulevard.
It's just a common everyday tree
An oak? An elm? Oh, fiddle-dee-dee.
It doesn't matter a tiny bit
What sort of a tree, so so-be-it!
This tree's important to habitat
Like bugs and birds and this and that.
They love to congregate on its bark
From dawn to dusk and even at dark.
Because you see I cover that tree
(At least one side, the one I can see)
With peanutbutter. Honest! It's true!
I swear up and down. May I turn blue
If I'm not telling the absolute truth!
And I've got pictures, if you need proof
That my old tree is covered weekly
With peanutbutter. And not sneak'ly!
Out I go with my long spatula
To spread it on, make it look naturala.
And then I run back to my old house
To see if chickadee or mouse
Comes up to taste this special treat
That I smear on that tree to eat!
And oh, they come! They are not shy!
Raccoons and skunks, birds from the sky!
I lovingly coat that tree with goo
So I can watch my private zoo
Climb up and fill their little bellies.
(I wonder; should I put out jellies?)

"STIRLING," A GOOD-BYE POEM
FOR ANDREW AND HUGH

Stirling lived with Andrew and Hugh
But in May '97 he died.
Their wondrous Scottie, so sweet, so true
Filled Andrew and Hugh's hearts with pride.
Andrew and Hugh will miss their dear friend,
But they gave him a life of such joy.
In time their broken hearts will mend
For Stirling, their dear little boy.

SANDS

You know how grains of sand
Keep shifting, changing and
Moving from beach to beach
By the ocean's hamm'ring reach
Starting out perhaps in Spain
And washing up on Bahrain?
Then centuries go by
And they end up on Shanghai
'Til the ocean's thund'rous roar
Pulls them to a cottage door
Built on Maine's rocky coast
Of stone and beam and post.
I spent my summers there
As a child, always aware
Of travelled grains of sand
Holding one in my hand
Wondering whence it came
Where was its last domain.
I think about the coasts
That ancient grain could boast

Of having seen and met
Then washed away to set
Upon another shore
It hadn't seen before.
I'm old and now remain
On that rock'd beach in Maine
And oft think of those grains
Of sand, and their terrains.
I wonder as I walk
If those sand grains could talk
I think that they might say
"Your feet this very day
"Are walking on the sands
"Which touched so many lands.
"Like you, those grains went far
"Came back, like Evening Star
"But some touched something more
"From years and years before.
"Your old bare feet are now
"Touching old grains somehow
"Your young feet touched back when
"You were a child, back then."

THE WHEELCHAIR

*Y*esterday I saw a curious sight
It was a man, sitting in the sunlight.
Now that in itself is not an odd thing
I've seen it done; it's not so amazing.
But this guy was sitting in his wheelchair
In a huge parking lot, in the bright air
Taking the sun, sitting there all alone
In his well-earned spot; the handicapped zone.

THERE IS JUST NO WAY

*I*t's impossible! I refuse to believe it!
There's just no way anyone could conceive it!
Even if God came down and insisted it's true
I still would not believe it. I mean come on, do you?
You do? Are you crazy? I mean think about it!
If you're a thinking person, you have got to doubt it!
After all the kadzillions of them? Even more?
After the kadzillions of years they've been out-of-door?
I'll never believe it, not in a kadzillion eons
And I'll tell the world, from emperors to peons
That every single one of those guys can take a hike
When they insist "No two snowflakes are ever alike."

HI THERE!

I'd love to know why
They always say "Hi!"
When they've only talked with you once.
They think you'll rejoice
At the sound of their voice
How can you remember the dunce?
You talked on the phone
Once to a Joan
About two or three years ago.
She rings up again
You answer and then
She chirps "Hi!" Then, in vacuo.
"Who is this? Inez?"
"Of course not!" she sez.
"I know me you recognize."
"Best say who you are,
"I don't have radar,"

I answer, contrariwise.
"And don't just say 'Hi!'
"Or I'll say 'good-bye!'
"I D yourself right now!
"Don't be so vain
"And such a pea-brain
"As to think I'd recall you somehow.
"I last heard you speak
"Years past! Not last week
"How could ever I recall you?
"I'm hanging up now
"And will bid you ciao
"So cheerio, you screwball you.
"Next time you call
"Get on the ball
"And say right away who you are.
"Don't just say 'Hi!'
"Unless you are my
"Old friend, OK? Au revoir."

THE BUS

She's packed all their lunches
And walked them in bunches
With shoutings and fuss
Off to the school bus.
    She trots quickly home
And though no gastronome
Yearns, as she runs
For hot coffee and buns.
    She pulls off her coat
And throws down her tote
Flops down in her chair
Runs her hands through her hair.
    She sighs with delight

And ignores the sight
Of strewn clothing and toys
Oh Joy! There's no noise!
     She opens the paper
Now quite past the nadir
She faces each morn
Getting children bus-born.
     She feels bliss complete
It goes sweet and deep
She's got the whole day
To clean up, and play!
     She wiggles her toes
And starts in to doze
When suddenly her head
Flies up. Oh, the dread!
     She hears the door open
(She's nervously hopin'
It's not what she thinks,)
And then her heart sinks.
     She sees her peace shattered
Her sweet plans now scattered
They pop like a bubble
She knows she's in trouble.
     She turns with a smile
(But it's fake, by a mile,)
All her kids have come back
Molly, Jim, Jane and Jack.
     She grits her teeth hard
Her brain a petard
And bites back the cuss
When she hears, "Missed the bus!"

SHOEHORN

Oh lord, I felt so old
She simply over me bowled
When I entered the shoe store.

I said "Is there a chance
"By any happenstance
"You might sell me a shoehorn?"

The sweet clerk stared at me
And then she said, "Oh gee,
"I'm sorry, but I'm new here.

"Do you know where they'd be?
"Would you describe for me
"How shoehorns do appear?"

I started to explain
But I felt just inane
Trying to define one.

And so I smiled and said
Just before I fled
"You'll know the day you find one."

The pretty clerk cried "Wait!
"Won't you demonstrate?
"Does one blow in a shoehorn?"

"Oh lord," I laughed out loud
(We'd begun to draw a crowd,)
I thought, "Is she a newborn?"

"No way!" I said to her
"No blowing! Oh no sir!
"A shoehorn's not a tuba!

"You use it to help slide
"Shoes which just won't glide
"On your feet when they get stook-a!"

"Oh," she said, perplexed
And I thought "Oh, what next?"
I again began to leave.

"Wait!" she called once more
And ran back to the store
But soon came back to me.

She handed me a gift
Held out in her fist.
She said "Please won't you take it?"

I looked up with surprise
And then tears filled my eyes
I just could not forsake it.

"Take it! It's for free!"
This sweet kid said to me
I really had to do it.

But just a jot beforn
She gave me the shoehorn
She put it to her mouth and blew it.

THE BABE

W hy does it always feel so fine
To make a baby at the time.
And why does it always feel so lousy
When it's time for that babe to come on outsy?

LACE DOILIES

*C*ould anything possibly look so fine
As the sight of lace doilies hanging out on a line?
It brings to my mind olden cozy things
Like lemonade and wicker, country fairs and brass rings
And antimacassars, pies and skittles
And old men talking softly midst the curls of their whittles.
Seeing white doilies swinging up high
Washed lovingly by hand and pinned up there to dry
And then taken down, starched, and put on plates
So things will look fetching like cookies or dates.
It's really a sight, so poignant, so fine,
Those bright white lace doilies drying out on a line.

VT.

I think there's a committee
To make all Vermont pretty.
I never see a single spot
Where it's ugly. Not a jot!
Oh I know it's got some grunge blots
That the group tries to expunge lots.
But they can't, so don't rebuke 'em
'Cause the committee plans to nuke 'em.
But Vermont, oh boy, it's splendid
I passionately recommend it
Beware though, if you trash it
You're likely to get bash-ed
By that very strict committee
Bent on keeping Vermont pretty.

Sophie My Friend

I watch her dancing night and day
In pirouette and plie.
Her tutu is spun golden net
She is a charming, sweet coquette.
I found her in an old doll shop
She swung and swirled, a cute snow-
drop.
All color, even brilliant shoes!
Swanlike, straining, lovely druse.
Her arms spread up in comely pose
Her legs spread wide, taut pointed toes.
High leaps through air she did with ease
She twirled and spun and danced the breeze.
Skinny was she? And pencil thin?
Graceful, doe-eyed, hair swanskin?
No, this dancer flying high
Was elderly, fat. No butterfly.
And did she dance straight through the air?
Yes she did, but to be fair
This ballerina opaline
Danced from the end of fishing line.
A tiny doll, but not portrayed
As youthful, fresh, a girlish maid.
She was chubby, old and tough
Made of cloth and other stuff.
Her hair was made of silken thread
And all were white upon her head.
Her legs were not like stems of reed
More like a case of overfeed.
Her waist did not resemble wasp's,
Her skin not warm, but more like frost.
She sagged, she flopped, she sure was old
But still a sight just to behold.

Chubby, strong and filled with hope
This ballet doll was not a dope.
Epitomizing hope eternal
She taught me we must keep life vernal.
I'd been too scared to start anew
I was too old, could not debut
A new career. "Oh no," I said.
"All that hard work will make me dead."
But then I saw that little doll
A ballerina was her call.
She said "I have to take a chance
To see, though old, that I can dance."
I hung her right above my chair
And loved the thought that she would dare
To try to learn a new pursuit
Her age? She didn't give a hoot.
I named her Sophie. She's my guide.
She taught me I should never hide
The wish that I could simply start
A new career dear to my heart.
Sophie spins and twirls in dance
Hung from her thread in jubilance.
She's old, obese and way past prime
But doesn't care! This is her time!
I gently swat, she spins askew
She and I, a pas de deux!
I look at her as I pursue
(Although I'm way past ingenue,)
My new career. Me? Obsolete?
Sure, I started past my peak
But so did Sophie. Look at her!
A ballerina! I concur
That we can start at any age
A new pursuit at any stage!
Who cares we're nigh the River Styx?
Old broads can still learn brand new tricks!

?

*W*ho am I?
Butterfly?
What am I?
Dragonfly?
Where am I?
Passerby?
Why am I?
Mystify.

SLIME-O

*O*nce upon a time
I saw a little slime
A-creepin' up on me.

Oh, what should I do
About this awful goo?
Would it try to eat me?

My feet froze to the floor
I couldn't reach the door
It oozed its way toward me.

I thought "this is a dream"
And started in to scream.
Oops, too late. It glugged me.

THE STEEPLEJACK

*A*nyone could see she loved that man up high
But he did not look down at her, that guy up in the sky.
But I knew that she loved him. I truly understood
As I watched that pretty girl in our neighborhood.
She was small and lithesome, and tended toward pink
    dresses
Her hair was long and yellow. (In olden days, "silk tresses.")
It was summer then; the young girl wore no shoes
Sun breezes tossed her hair and lit her eyes with druse.
I said "Why do you watch him every single day?"
She stared at me and finally said "I have to find a way.
"But, I don't know you, never met you. So why do you ask?"
"Oh please," I said, "forgive me, but every day I've
    passed,
"I see you watching him up there and I wonder why."
I really had to know why she stared up at his sky.
The sweet girl dropped her eyelids then and I could see a
    tear
Slide slowly down upon her cheek, crystal-like and clear.
She looked at me and tried to smile and started in to
    speak
But choked a bit and when she spoke, her voice was soft
    and meek.
"I follow him to all his jobs with hopes he'll notice me
"But he's so high and I'm so low and I can't make him see
"That I'm down here awaiting him. And he just passes by
"When he comes down. I try to speak, but all I do is sigh."
I looked up at the man she loved, and wondered how she
    could
Fancy this odd steeplejack. What if he were no good?
Even from my viewpoint I saw this young man clear
He was a comely lad, a man who had no fear
Of soaring heights and sun and gales and birds and bees
    and rain

I thought "to do that job up there, he's got to be insane!"
His hair was yellow, just like hers, his muscles thick and
    taut
His legs were long, tanned arms were strong, he was a
    juggernaut.
I looked back at the sweet young girl. She smiled way up
    at him
And I could tell she thought he was one of the seraphim.
I heard some music from on high, strange and sweet and
    pure
I looked to see the source of it and then I knew for sure.
It floated from that boy above, for taped to his platform
He had a radio there for him, his music was skyborn.
And as it played he hummed along, his voice was deep
    and mellow
And sometimes he would sing some words; his voice was
    like a cello.
The tanned young man swung back and forth, he wore an
    old straw hat
He transformed that old steeple with paint and love
    thereat.
He loved his job and it was clear he had great love for
    spires
And churches too. So this boy was the one they always
    hired
To do the job. He could be trusted always to fulfill
His obligations for that job for which he had such skill.
The days passed on, the steeplejack continued with his job
The sweet young girl continued too, to watch her dear
    heartthrob.
Then late one day as his job slowed, the young man by
    mistake
Cut the tape which held his radio. He knew that it would
    break
When it fell down onto the street. That radio would
    smash.

And then his source of music would just be only trash.

He watched it fall down toward the street and saw it spin
and whirl

But then to his great horror, it landed on the girl.

It hit her head and knocked her down. The steeplejack
screamed "No!"

Then he rappelled down to her side and shouted
"Someone! Go!

"Please! Call an ambulance for this lovely wounded lass!

"My radio has killed her. I think her brains are bashed."

He then knelt down beside her and pulled her body close

And stared at her unconscious face and thought "she is
the most

"Lovely creature I have seen. Where has she been til
now?"

And then he heard the sirens wail, and finally did allow

The men to come and pick her up and put her on the
stretcher.

And one kind medic said to him, "Don't worry son, I'll
betcha

"She'll be fine. I've seen much worse. We'll take the best
of care.

"You want to come and ride with her? We think it's only
fair,

"Since 'cause of you she got this way, so you should real-
ly go

"To hospital with her. You'll see it through, I know."

The steeplejack's name was Tom, the young girl's name
was June

And hat pushed back, he held her hand and soft began to
croon.

His voice, just like it was on high, was hushed and sweet
and mellow

And June responded slightly to that voice so like a cello.

The steeplejack sat by her sickbed every day

And gently held her hand and each day he would pray.

He'd also sing to June, she slept her coma through.
And as she had before, he thought he saw her move.
"I'm sorry, dear sweet June," Tom whispered through his
    tears
"I've only just found out you've loved me for some years.
"A woman told me that. She said you always stood
"Below me as I worked. Who knew? The likelihood
"Of someone sweet like you watching me each day
"I just could not believe. I don't know what to say!
"Oh June, you've loved me long while I was high above
"I never saw you there. I never felt your love.
"I never looked below. The sky is where I thrive,
"I love it way up there. It's where I feel alive!
"I paint and fix the steeples, and play my music too
"What better life than that? But now, dear June, there's
    you.
"Seeing you each day, knowing why you're here
"Makes me think that I must always keep you near.
"I wish you'd spoken out when I came down each eve
"But I know that you're shy, and young and so naive.
"I pray that you will wake, my darling little girl
"There is so much to say, my head is all a-whirl.
"To see you sleeping there makes my heart ache with
    pain
"It's my fault that you're here, I couldn't pre-ordain
"That this could really happen, but now because it has
"I think I've finally found my love. I'm happy! But alas,
"You can't wake up and I don't know if you will ever see me
"Or if we'll speak or love or play, or if you'll e'er redeem
    me."
He lay his head down by her side and wept some more
    that night
And slept a while and then stood up and reached to shut
    the light.
"Tom?" he heard, the sound was soft, but still it shocked
    him deep.

And "Tom?" again, and Tom stood still. He felt his sore
　　heart beat.
"Is it you? Are you back?" the young man nearly wept.
Her eyes were wide, her lips a-smile. He stared, could not
　　accept
That June awoke and spoke to him. Then joy spread
　　through his soul!
"Yes, I'm back" she grinned at him. Her hair was marigold.
Her eyes were blue, like skies in fall, her lips were bright
　　and pink
Her body full, her face just glowed. All Tom could do was
　　blink.
And finally, when his breath came back, he said "You are
　　my life.
"I know how you have waited, June, so now, please, be
　　my wife!"
And pretty June stared up at him, his face was very near.
Her heart was full, she said to him "Oh Tom, my darling
　　dear,
"May I go to the sky with you?" she asked her startled
　　swain
"To the steeples with me, dear? In wind and sun and
　　rain?"
"Yes my darling," June said clear. "Please do teach me
　　how
"To fix the steeples, just like you, to be together now
"And every day. We'll work together up there in the sky!"
"Well, yes!" he laughed, "I can do that. Together! You and I
"Up atop the world we two, what a team indeed!"
June grinned at Tom and said, "I have one other need."
"What's that, beloved June," said Tom. "Your wish is my
　　desire."
"I want," she said, "for us to marry while swinging from a
　　spire.
"I want for us to marry in a sunset's wondrous glow
"And wave to all our cherished friends cheering us below.

"While roped to a great steeple, I want to say our vows
"And we will use old fashioned words like 'promise, thee's
    and thou's.'"
"I want," said June, "the two of us to wed while in the air
"Can you find a preacher who'd marry us up there?"
"Oh yes!" laughed Tom. "I've just the man. He'll do the job
    for sure."
"Oh Tom!" sighed June, "I really could not ever ask for
    more.
"Oh June, my June," cried Tom, "Imagine! Married close
    to God!
"But June, you haven't answered me!" Tom said with
    mournful nod.
"We've all these plans and I'm so thrilled, but you have
    not agreed
"To marry me my darling girl, oh June, say yes, I plead!"
She'd waited for this dear young man, her steeplejack, for-
    ever
And now he was right here with her, planning life together.
"Dear Tom," she smiled, "I've loved you long, so surely
    you can guess
"Marry you? Who loves the sky? Oh yes, dear Tom. Oh
    yes!"

FRANK'S OBSESSION

*W*e have this friend named Frank who has a favorite word
And as a city person, it's one I'd never heard.
He always somehow manages to find a way to use it
(And frankly, Frank, I have to say, you pretty much abuse
    it.)
Now Frank has always shown that he's a real bright man
Honestly, he'd have to be, since only this man can
Work this crazy word into every conversation
Causing all who hear it to feel major 'zasperation.

He's hooked on this odd word, and by now, it's quite
  enough.
We wish from his vocabulary he would off it slough.
It's really quite astonishing how our friend Frank can make
This word come up so often. It just makes my head shake.
The man has gone to college, has earned tons of degrees
His IQ is so high, it's nothing to over sneeze.
I hate to take a car trip in the country with that man
'Cause then for sure he'll say that word, as usual deadpan.
He never seems to notice how we look at him askance
When that damned word comes up, that madd'ning utter-
  ance.
And uh-oh, when we pass a farm, Frank lights up like a
  lamp
'Cause now he'll have a reason; at repeating, Frank's a
  champ.
I see a farm ahead of us, the silo tall and red
I see Frank's eyes light brightly, I see him raise his head.
I see him smile, I hear him say "Oh those guys have the
  best!"
I groan and turn my head away. There's no point to
  protest.
For Frank can work that word into any dialogue
At cocktail parties, Broadway plays, while eating a hot
  dog.
I know you'll think it's awfully queer when I tell you this
  word
You'll wonder why he uses it, you'll think he's just absurd.
It's just not ever fitting, and it makes no sense whatever
He's joined to this weird word and simply can't dissever.
I'll tell you what it is now; you'll cock your head in doubt
You'll wonder what on earth Frank is really all about.
So here it is, it's odd that Frank can get so darned much
  mileage
Out of this word, it's inane! The word he loves is "silage."

SUZY FREEMAN'S QUILTS

The sights were dazzling on that diamond summer day
As we drove through the countryside loving the sight
Of shining trees, farms, and hills. The day a nosegay
Of scents and sounds and views, and warm, flooding sun-
    light.

Everything was perfect. We were very happy
And we sang along with the radio, old songs.
We loved their melodic lyrics, sweet and snappy.
And we laughed together, he and I, the day long.

And when we saw all those quilts hanging from the trees
And the sign saying "Suzy Freeman's Quilts for sale"
And saw them snap and sway and ripple in the breeze
And saw how glorious they looked swinging, skysale

We had to stop to view these fabric jewels and so
We did. Suzy herself sat quilting in the shade
Proud her quilts were putting on such a joyful show
For folks driving by. And she loved the accolade

Offered by people when they stopped. She loved to talk
And loved to show her home and tell about her life.
She'd stand, extend her hand and say "look and walk!"
And she'd tell her story. She'd had her share of strife.

Ancient, like a settler's place, Suzy's weathered home
Was heated with wood, and lights were from kerosene.
Hands worn, like old leather, her face a wrinkled poem
Her age? Sixty through ninety, something in between.

Suzy's quilts were wondrous, thick, soft and so well made
We bought three, and couldn't wait to take them back
    home.

On our bed, one looked like ruby, sapphire, and jade
Like spilled cloth jewels, vibrant, colorful fabric poem.

We slept beneath it that first night and it was warm
And it all but glowed in the moonlight in our room.
But in the night we knew something was not the norm.
Something was wrong with that quilt we had to assume.

It began to itch us dreadfully and then more,
Tiny slivers of sticks and stuff and more sharp things
Began to work their ways up through the cloth, like spore.
The quilt soon felt like a briar patch. Amazing!

More and more stuff came out of Suzy's creation
Bugs and creepy crawlies and stuff not meant for quilts
Should we keep Suzy's glorious origination?
I'd much rather walk barefoot forever on stilts.

THE WALKING GUY

*H*e walks and walks and walks, that guy
His car is the color of the sky
His eyes are blue, I saw them too
(I looked at him as he passed by.)

For years he's parked his sky blue car
Out in the country, way, afar
And then he'd walk for miles and miles
From dawn sometimes, to evening star.

I don't know why that guy will walk
(He never ever stops to talk.)
Perhaps his doctor told him to
(Perhaps he thought he oughtn't balk!)

I see his car parked everywhere
Where there are trees and pure, fresh air
His head is down, he wears a frown
An old red hat covers up his hair.

I wonder if he has a job
And if he does, I find it odd
That he can amble all day long
(Does he get money straight from God?)

Years and years and years have passed
And as years go, they've gone real fast
But still I see that sky-blue car
And still he walks, his eyes downcast.

His coat? It's still the same old brown
His shoes? They look the same; worn down.
He bends now lower as he walks
Out in the country, town to town.

When I go driving anywhere
I see him parked. He's everywhere!
His car's sky blue. His eyes are too.
That walking guy is off somewhere.
       But where?

FOREST BUGS

*W*hen I take a stroll through the woods and thousands of
    insects swarm at me out of the air
I'm instantly curious about something and it's this; what
    do they eat when I'm not there?

SweetieDearyHoneyDarlin'

I just wish I knew the name of that fool
The dimwit who made up that stupid rule
That calling a woman "Honey" or "Dear"
Is some sort of insult, something to jeer.
I want to confess it's something I like
(Though my fellow (!) sisters'd say "take a hike!")
They'd also deride me and say with scorn
"Please tell us, where in the world were you born?
"Some backward country where women wear veils?
"Hey now, we're emancipated females!"
I know that, I do! I'm liberated too!
But that doesn't mean that I must eschew
Men who say "Sweetie" and "Dearie" and such
Really, to make a scene is just too much.
These feminists warn us, they scold and chide
That if we allow that, we have no pride.
They warn us loudly, their voices keening
That men shouldn't do that, it's demeaning.
To whom? Me or them? I just don't get it.
They ought to relax, try not to sweat it.
Now for me, those terms just make me grin.
They're great! They get kinda under my skin.
I like them! They're nice, they make me feel good
So I guess I'm sacked from the Sisterhood.
You know, maybe men who call us that
Don't mean it to sound like a foul fiat
Sometimes they just can't remember our names
(And they'd never use terms like "broads" or "dames.")
I don't think when men call us "darlin'" or "Hon"
We ought to contemplate getting a gun
Or haul them away to the guillotine
Or attack them with a hammer ball peen
Or draw and quarter them like a loathed foe
Or deliver them a fierce body blow

Or have them imprisoned, throwing the key
Into a canyon, or into the sea.
Come on, it's really not such a big deal
Using those terms doesn't make man a heel.
Now if a kid did it, while bagging my food
I'd quite quickly squelch that boy's attitude.
But when a nice man is fixing my sink
And once calls me "Dear," I won't make a stink
Or if a guy driving me to my train
Asks "how's it goin', hon?" I'd be insane
To call him a lout when he meant no harm
And frankly, you know? It kind of has charm.
So what's all the fussing, can you tell me?
Do those feminists have to make a decree?
When I hear those names, I'll feel no rancor
'Cause I'm a proud woman with no need to roar.